The $500 Wedding

How to have a beautiful wedding and reception for $500

By Heather Henry Kraabel

The $500 Wedding: How to have a beautiful wedding and reception for $500

By Heather Henry Kraabel

ISBN 978-0-6152-3797-8

Dedicated to the Henry's, the Kraabel's, and my husband Nick

TABLE OF CONTENTS

INTRODUCTION

When planning a wedding, it is important to remember that you have now entered a world of chaos where people shower you freely with their opinions and good-natured suggestions on everything from the month you marry to dinner music. Taffeta and tulle surround you at every turn, your schedule resembles that of a fulltime New York City event planner, and money is now a four letter word that is used by even decent folks like your grandmother. A simple decision regarding your wedding dress could disappoint everyone from your mother to your second cousin (who isn't even engaged yet but swears that was the dress *she* was going to buy.)

What is a bride or groom to do? You can't please everyone and there comes a point where this thing is just going to happen so stop bugging me already and let's just get married! Gosh! Ok, take a deep breath, things really aren't that bad. Let's go back and start from the beginning...

First of all, it goes without saying that weddings are expensive. Maybe your parents are going to help you with the cost, maybe you have a little money saved up, or maybe you plan on throwing the whole thing on your credit cards and pay off the debt with the money you'll receive as gifts from your friends and family. Yeah, that seems like a really good idea.

If you want an easy way to reduce stress and really enjoy everything your wedding day should be, then follow the tips in this book. You'll find out there are three things you can do right now, from the moment you're engaged, to diminish your stress level *significantly*.

Why do we always fight about money?

All we did was fight about how much everything cost, if I brought home a bag from the craft store or the department store, I'd have explain how much it cost and why we needed it. Every time a new detail would pop up, we'd be stressed instead of excited because we'd have to figure out where the money would come from. I kept thinking "Isn't planning a wedding supposed to be fun?"

A lot of us fight about money because money represents much more than just a dollar amount. Many of us see money as a representation of how successful we are, what we do for a living, an indication of how far we've come, a sense of stability, and a source of power. Topics like who makes more money or who will pay for what can lead to crazy fights that will strain relationships.

Weddings are extremely vulnerable to fights over money because weddings involve so many different people in a family and when you feel that people you love are under fire, your reaction will likely be aggressive. In fact, when you start your marriage with strife and conflict with family members because of money issues surrounding your wedding day, those bad feelings could linger on for years, and who wants to fight about the cost of your bouquet three years later during Thanksgiving dinner?

Let's put this all into perspective; ask yourself these questions:

- Am I willing to put myself, my partner, or my family in debt to pay for an expensive wedding?

- Does my need to have lavish wedding details outweigh my need to have a peaceful and meaningful wedding celebration?

- What kind of financial strain would an expensive wedding put on those I love?

- If I have money saved up, should I use all of it to pay for an extravagant wedding?

- What details of my wedding day are really important and what things are not as important?

- At the end of my wedding day, will I be any less married if spend $500 versus $15,000?

Even if you have more than $500 to spend

The tips in this book can save you so much time, stress, and headache. Take it from those of us who have had to plan a wedding; stress and exhaustion can turn what's supposed to be one of the happiest days of your life into a day that you're just praying you will live through.

My wedding day almost reminds me of the way I used to feel every year around Christmas time. I tried so hard ahead of time to get all of the things on my to-do list done so that I could really sit back and enjoy the holiday. I got my Christmas cards out early, I did my shopping online, we decorated the day after Thanksgiving, I even started buying groceries months ahead of time.

However, no matter what, I was always crazy busy with little time to sit back and enjoy the real meaning of Christmas. Every single year I vowed that I'd make this Christmas season less stressful, but that just never seemed to happen.

In recent years, things have gotten much better though. We have finally begun to say no to the things we felt we were obligated to do in years past and we're finally learning to ask for help in the areas where we really needed help (like having guests bring some of the food, or putting a spending limit on gifts, etc.) Now, I try to get everything I possibly can done by December 15th which gives me ten full days to just sit back with my hot cocoa, watch the snow fall, and appreciate everything the season has to offer.

This is the same mentality we're applying to planning your wedding. Make a list, stick to your budget, ask for help, use your resources, and keep things very neat and simple. And always allow yourself time to take a deep breath and soak in the moment; you're getting married!

So if you have more than $500 to spend, that's great! However, the tips and ideas in this book will still help you minimize the stress and expense and maximize the wonderful memories your wedding day should give you.

And think about the numbers a bit, if you've got a budget of $2000 and you spend only $500, that's $1500 you could put towards a honeymoon or new furniture or a puppy!

THE BUDGET

*We got engaged and I was so excited! I knew we didn't
have a lot of money but I figured we'd get it somewhere.
Then we started planning and the costs just added up fast.
I realized that we were either going to start our life with a
large amount of debt or get married at the court house and
order a pizza for the reception.*

A lot of people feel this way. The book is titled *The $500
Wedding*, but it's not just about how much money you'll be
spending on your big day, it's also about simplifying an
event that has been complicated by so many for so many
generations. If ever there was proof that money doesn't
make you happy, it's a wedding. No matter how much
money you may have to spend on the day, you are
undoubtedly going to be stressed and exhausted even
before it starts. Your honeymoon, if you have any money
left over to take one, will feel more like rehab then a
vacation. So forget about borrowing a bunch of money
from your parents, don't apply for three more credit cards,
and don't spend your entire savings. Just don't do it.
Instead, pull together $500 and let's plan a beautiful
wedding that you'll actually enjoy. This isn't to say that a
wedding should be some half-baked idea that you threw
together at the last minute. Weddings are beautiful and
precious memories. Spending money on them isn't
wasteful or irresponsible. However, spending $50,000 on a
wedding isn't possible for a lot of us and we shouldn't feel
guilty about that. If you want to save money because you
don't have a lot of money, or you'd rather put your extra

money into a home or a vacation, or you really don't want to borrow more than you feel comfortable paying back than consider the $500 budget laid out for you in this book.

Let's establish some rules and why they're important. The following rules are crucial because they dictate the entire theme of planning your wedding. You are more than likely going to be tempted to spend money, especially if you let yourself play those mind games like, "Well, how many times does a person get married?" or "It's my wedding, I want to treat myself to something nice." You absolutely should but always keep the rules in mind.

The three rules that you must stick to in order to pull off a wedding budget of $500 or less:

- Plan a small and intimate affair

- Borrow, borrow, and borrow

- Use every resource you have

If you want nothing less than a huge event in a large cathedral with twelve bridesmaids, a string quartet, and a horse-drawn carriage- this may not be the book for you. But if you pick fifty people who you love most in the world and invite them to a candle-lit ceremony with an intimate reception where people can enjoy the food, company, and celebration of the day; then you can definitely have that and a lot more for less than $500.

Our budget is broken down into the traditional categories; we're just going to follow the three rules. We'll apply them to the guest list, the wedding reception, your attire, the photographs, the music, the flowers, *everything*.

A skeleton of your budget will look something like this:

Wedding Dress	$100
Groom's Attire	$25
Accessories	$10
Flowers	$15
Photographs	$50
Music	$10
Food/Drink	$220
Decorations	$20
Invitations	$30
Miscellaneous*	$20
TOTAL →	**$500**

* You want a miscellaneous category for any last minute things that pop up on the day of your wedding.

I'm guessing you're probably thinking this is impossible, it isn't impossible but does require all of your creativity and resourcefulness. Later, I'll show you some actual weddings with a budget of $500 and we'll look at exactly where the money went. But right now we need to get real about how we're going to make this $500 wedding budget dream a reality. For example, how in the world are we going to find a beautiful wedding dress for just $100?

Never turn away help

As soon as people found out my boyfriend and I were getting married, I was getting offers to help from everyone. I couldn't believe it! Some of my coworkers offered to lend me jewelry, one of my aunts asked if there was any food she could make or bring for the reception, and my cousin volunteered to make the invitations!

I was always amazed at the number of people who upon finding out I was planning my wedding would say, "Wow, do you need any help?" Automatically I would almost always respond with "Oh no, thank you but I think we've got it under control." Why say that? There was no way I had it under control, in fact the day before my wedding I spent about sixteen hours just running errands. I'm not kidding, I was all over town that day trying to finish last minute tasks and I had almost nobody for help. I was so stressed out, I was exhausted, and I ended up being an hour late to the groom's dinner.

If you want to save money and feel less stressed about your wedding day, you are going to need help. Make a list of all of the things you need, I'm talking every little detail from hemming your dress to making the frosting on your wedding cake, and write it down. Keep that list with you at all times and when someone asks you if you need help, say something like, "That would be great, I know you have a great music collection, would you mind letting me borrow some of your music for the reception?" And just like that, your music problem is solved and it's crossed off your list. Just make sure you are keeping your partner or anyone else helping you plan the wedding informed so that you are all working from the same to-do list.

So get thinking of people who could help you and then start asking them. Is your aunt talented with a sewing machine? Ask her if she can help you with dress alterations. Is your sister's makeup flawless? Ask her to do your makeup for the wedding. Who do you know with a green thumb? Ask them if they could help you decorate with flowers and plants. Who's a wiz on the computer? Could they help make your invitations? Can you borrow some serving dishes from your grandmother? Can your uncle take pictures at the wedding and reception? Can someone pick up the wine and flowers for you? How about servers?

Brainstorm some ideas about who wouldn't mind getting dressed and playing caterer for a day. Sometimes your teenage cousins who are otherwise vulnerable to boredom at family gatherings wouldn't mind stepping up to the challenge. (Plus their parents will be there to make sure they're aren't goofing off or drinking all of your wine.)

Your to-do list will be huge and will likely grow larger everyday, so start working on it and start asking for help...*today.*

Where to "shop"

The word shop in this section means where to borrow. You have ample resources at your fingertips; you just need to know where to look.

First, look to your friends. Because we don't want to make people feel used or slighted, stick to only the friends that will be invited to your wedding. Maybe you know some friend of a friend that you one time hung out with at a happy hour. That's probably not a good resource even though you know for a fact that she has the perfect necklace to go with your dress. Look to your good friends and lay out the facts for them: You're working with a tight budget and you need their help. You'll likely be given full access to their jewelry box and closet but make sure you also ask them to keep their eyes open for any great deals they come across during their own trips to the mall.

If you put the notice out there that you're looking for a great deal and list the specific items you're looking for, most friends will be happy to help. Just make sure you plan some way to thank them for their help. Maybe after the wedding is over and you're settled a bit, you can have your biggest helpers over for a nice dinner. Anything that lets them know you appreciate everything they've done to make your special day a reality.

Second, look to your future husband/wife. Most women I know who are planning a wedding take on almost all of the duties themselves. Maybe your guy isn't into the planning and that's okay however, if he knows someone who is a good singer or a good cook, he needs to let you know. The easiest way to get your significant other to help out is right away ask them what's important to them. They probably don't care one bit what kind of flowers you carry down the aisle but they might care a lot about what song is played. If they're leaving everything up to you, make another list detailing what duties are best suited for them. Like, arranging transportation from the church to the reception or finding someone to tape the ceremony. Find some duty for everyone or you'll be even more stressed during an already stressful time.

Third, look to your parents (and your future in-laws!). Take inventory of what your family has that might be useful during the wedding ceremony or reception. It's quite likely that your parents will enjoy some family possessions involved in the festivities since it's a family occasion. Of course you'll be careful with anything extremely valuable but what's the point of having something like china dishes if you're never going to use them?

Also, think about jewelry. You know the something old, something new, something borrowed, something blue thing... your mother's jewelry is old and borrowed! Are there any great earrings or necklaces in her collection? What about Dad? Does he have any cuff links that could be borrowed or maybe even a nice suit jacket?

Be creative and think about every possible thing you could borrow and then just ask. The worse thing that happens is that someone says no and that's okay. Just be resourceful and open-minded about what you can use to achieve the beautiful wedding you want.

AT THE END OF THE BOOK, THERE IS A BUDGET WORKSHEET FOR YOU TO FILL OUT WITH YOUR PERSONALIZED BUDGET. I STRONGLY RECOMMEND USING PENCIL.

THE GUEST LIST

I had no idea what I was going to do. Counting just our relatives, our guest list was over a hundred people! There was no way we were going to be able to afford to pay for a dinner with that many people!

This task can be fun and it can be painful. You'll need to figure out who's going to be there and who isn't and it's not always a clear decision. Feelings can get hurt and you don't want to disappoint your parents or your future in-laws.

The best way to handle the guest list is by right away telling people you want a small and intimate wedding. Use language that is clear about what kind of wedding you're envisioning and people will likely get the message that not everyone you know and like will be there. It's close friends and family only. If people know that right away, there's going to be less pressure on you to invite others because you fear they might feel left out. You won't have the burden of thinking about which coworkers to invite, or whether or not your second cousins should be there.

I just had a really good friend of mine say he was thinking about asking his girlfriend to marry him. Jokingly I said, do you want me to be an usher? Right away he laughed and said no, they had talked about having a small wedding on the beach in Mexico and then maybe a reception later for friends and extended family. Just like that, the plan was clear and even though I wouldn't get offended about the guest list anyway, he let me know right away that it was probably just going to be close family at the ceremony. It's just that simple.

It is an unbelievable savings if you can keep the guest list at fifty people or less. You'll save money on food, invitations, programs, table space, drinks, and a lot more. You might think at first that this is an impossible task, especially if you have a large family. My husband and I both had mothers who were one of seven children. By the time we invited all of the aunts and uncles and cousins on mothers' sides alone, we were way over fifty people so I completely understand how hard this task can be. But it is possible. If your families are huge, then how about just sticking to your immediate family members, your godparents, grandparents, and really close friends. If none of the aunts, uncles, and cousins are coming, there shouldn't be any hurt feelings. They've already been informed that you want something small and intimate and they're likely to understand because they belong to the same huge family, and small and intimate does not include everyone in the family tree.

Also, there's nothing that says you can't have a post-wedding day gathering where your extended family can celebrate your big day. What about planning the next big holiday, like Christmas or New Year's, with all of the relatives invited? A nice dinner, a chance to show off the wedding pictures, and a chance to actually celebrate with each other instead of talking to your relatives for five minutes in the receiving line. There are people who came to my wedding that I really wanted to talk to and catch up with but because of the amount of guests, I was lucky if I got to say hi to everyone much less have a conversation with them. It may be a lot more meaningful for you to sit down with your aunts and uncles, show them the video, talk about the day and make them feel that it was never a slight against them to keep the guest list short, it was just something that was important to you and your budget.

Those of you, who have a smaller family, take advantage of that. After your family members have been invited, you'll have to narrow down the friends. But people almost always understand and will not be offended if they don't receive an invite if you let them know that you're having an intimate celebration. You can start trimming the list by putting everyone into group one or group two. Group one people are your definitely-must-be-there people and group two people are the people who are optional. The word optional sounds harsh, but no one's going to know what list they were on unless you and your partner show them and why would you do that? Also, just because Group two is optional doesn't mean they're less important, it's just a necessary move in order to keep costs low.

We decided after many stressful conversations that we had to keep our guest list small. And after we accepted that, everything seemed to run smoother. Suddenly, we had more money to spend on the details that were important to us for our wedding. We were also surprised at how understanding everyone was. We thought for sure there would be a lot of drama about who was and wasn't on the guest list, but there was none!

After you've made the two lists, start eliminating as many people as possible from group two. Fifty people might be an unattainable number for you, but limit your guest list as much as you possibly can; close family and friends *only*. What's important is the enjoyment that you and your partner get out of the day. After all, it's a celebration of the two of you starting a new life together, not a tally of how many people you each know and like.

How to keep your Guest List small

We didn't know where to start! Would we actually cut out aunts and uncles? My coworkers? His old roommates? I was so tense about the guest list that it made the rest of the wedding planning impossible to be excited about.

Leave out the coworkers and neighbors

crazy neighbors from two doors down. So they know you're getting married, so what? You are not obligated to invite them because your families happened to find homes they liked on the same block years ago or because they always gave you great candy on Halloween when you were a kid. I realize that neighbors can become good friends but you don't want to fall into that "invitation by association" routine; like if you invite the Hanson's then you have to invite the Murphy's. Skip all neighbors and apply the same rule to coworkers. Some coworkers might be close friends so of course, their name may be on the list. Just remember to limit your wedding talk at work to avoid hurting anyone's feelings. Just remember the rule: Family and *close* friends only.

Don't feel guilty about not inviting everyone you like

This is a wedding celebration not an episode of "This is your Life." We know your good friend from high school who you haven't seen in years would have a blast at your wedding and reception but if you want to stick with your budget, you have to put these people in the optional list.

Keep in mind, if people hear you're having a small wedding, most people will know that means just family and a few friends.

If you haven't talked to someone in a year, they are in Group Two (or maybe just cut)

They can still be your best friend from grade school, they can still be your old college roommate, but if you haven't talked to them for awhile then chances are they are not classified as a close friend and shall therefore be placed in the optional list. Plus, if you haven't talked to them in a year, they may not know many people at the wedding which will make it harder for them to relax and have a good time. This could make it harder for you to relax and have a good time.

Think twice about brand new friends

This whole guest list formation can seem cruel at times but it's not about whom you like, it's about what size of a wedding you really want or need. People who you've met and become friends just recently might seem like people you should invite (especially if you've been talking with them a lot about your wedding) but let's think about it carefully. They are probably not going to know very many people there, it might make older friends wonder why they were cut before the new friends, and you aren't going to have tons of time on your big day to make sure that the new friends in your circle are comfortable and having a good time.

Also, this is a dangerous area because you start adding on the "association" invites. For example, you may feel pressure to invite people just because of who they are associated with. I had a good friend who was a bridesmaid in my wedding and occasionally I would hang out with her roommates. When it came time to put together my guest list, I stressed out about whether I should invite them or not. I decided against it and one of them showed up anyway. Then I felt awkward when I saw her knowing that she wasn't really on the guest list to begin with but since she was associated with one of my close friends, she had assumed she was invited. It was uncomfortable and could have been avoided if I had made it clear early on that we were having a small wedding.

Telling people it's a small wedding seems to be the code word that lets everyone know (without being rude) that you have decided to only have a few family and friends there. People seem to get it when you use those words. If you say things like, "we're trying to keep our numbers down" or "we're trying not to let our guest list get out of control" it often doesn't get the point across.

Again, repeat this in your head: Close friends and family only. Close friends and family only.

Unless your parents are paying for it, don't invite their friends to the celebration

You are going to have a hard enough time making room for your own close friends so unless you have no other choice, your parent's friends do not have to be there. These are classic examples of people who are wonderful people but nevertheless belong on the optional list.

I know this can be tough because sometimes these people are like an extension to your own family but unless they are very close friends of *yours*, they need to be on the optional list.

Make the whole thing "adults only"

This might make sense anyways if you're going to have an evening wedding or a court house ceremony. The easiest way to do this is to specifically list the names of the adults and not the children. To make sure the message gets through, have a polite relative help you spread the word.

If having a no-kids celebration seems rude, there are still plenty of ways to include the kids without and save money. Think about setting aside a special meal for them instead of what you're serving the adults. Chances are peanut butter and jelly sandwiches with chips and lemonade will be more popular for them anyway but also it's cheaper for you.

You can also save money by letting the kids use paper plates and of course, you don't have to worry about them drinking alcohol so that will help your budget and party planning too. Kids can also help you clean up or entertain your guests before dinner. Maybe they can take some pictures or older kids can even help serve food or fill the water glasses. Kids like to feel important and know that they are doing something to help.

Use an early RSVP date on your invitations

That way, if anyone from your "must-have" list can't be there, you can grab someone from the optional list and have enough time to send them an invite without it being awkward.

All around, an early RSVP date helps you because it just lets you know what kind of party and what size of party you'll have which is key when you're working with a tight budget.

Do you need to invite your second or third cousins or your great aunts and uncles?

No. People will probably expect to see your aunts and uncles there, they probably won't expect your parent's aunts and uncles to be there. Neither will your parent's aunts and uncles. Again, *close* family and friends only!

Besides, how dumb will you feel if you can't remember their name and you haven't sent them a Christmas card ever and they haven't seen you since you were four years old. You've got good friends that were left off the list who will likely be friends with you for life. Let's not let a family tree take down this wedding budget.

Don't put "and guest" on the invites when inviting a single person

It's okay for them to come to the wedding alone, and sometimes it's easier for them anyway. Besides, if they are a close friend or relative (as everyone on your guest list should be), they will know everyone there and will not feel uncomfortable about being at your wedding alone.

Think about it like this too: You had to cut some people from your list that you really cared about but just didn't have the money to invite. Is it fair that ten strangers come to your wedding now because they are friends with your friends?

Don't worry so much about being rude or keeping up with appearances. Having a small wedding isn't rude, it's elegant. Besides, trying to keep up with whatever everyone else is doing will break your budget very quickly.

Don't forget yourself

If you're trying to limit your budget and you're thinking about the cost per person when determining a food budget: Do not forget yourself or the groom when figuring the final cost. A lot of people do that so a good rule of thumb is to always put you and your partner on the top of every list, then your parents, then everyone else.

Remember, it's all about letting everyone know from the start what your plan is. If everyone knows right away that you're planning a small wedding they are less likely to expect an invite. You'll deal with less hurt feelings and less expectations. Call relatives personally if you think it will make things smoother. Plan that after wedding dinner to let everyone know that they're still very important to you. Some people have big weddings, some people have small weddings, some people elope, some people get married at the court house, some people get married on a cruise ship; everyone's different.

SEE THE END OF THIS BOOK FOR SPACE WHERE YOU CAN START WORKING ON YOUR GUEST LIST. USING A PENCIL IS STRONGLY RECOMMENDED.

THE INVITATIONS

A friend of mine who was engaged and getting married about two months before me and my boyfriend sent her invitations in custom envelopes with personalized stamps. While they were beautiful, I knew that they must have been extremely expensive. Our invites were very simple and actually homemade. As I added up the approximate cost of my friend's invite, I was so thankful that we had put our money into other details of the wedding and reception.

This is a necessary expense, no way around it. But we don't need all of the frills that are very unnecessary and go unnoticed by everyone. Spend your money on the things guests will notice and the things they will truly appreciate- like the food at the reception. You can have wonderful invitations that are truly beautiful yet inexpensive.

Also keep in mind, this is where your smaller guest list comes in and saves you big bucks. If you estimate fifty guests at 42 cents per stamp, that's $21. If you spend two dollars on envelopes and ten dollars on some specialty paper and make the invites on your own computer, the cost of your invitations comes to $33. You can save money on stamps by delivering some of the invites yourself which will bring that $33 down to $30. Furthermore, don't double your postage costs with pre-stamped RSVP cards, just include a phone number or email address for guests to respond to the invite. Maybe even get a free website from Yahoo or MySpace where your guests can RSVP and also see pictures of you and your partner, find directions to the church, locate a nearby hotel, etcetera.

Here are some creative invitation ideas to get you inspired:

Stationary

If you don't mind doing a little leg work, spend an afternoon combing through craft stores, business supply stores, and discount stores for stationary. You can find some really beautiful prints and papers on sale and they usually come in packs of at least eight. Business supply stores will be more likely to carry larger packs. But the wonderful thing about stationary is that it comes with matching envelopes, lovely prints, and are easily adaptable to your personal computer. Simply adjust the margins on your page layout, do a practice print on plain white computer print, then go crazy with your invitations. You are only limited by imagination.

Things to keep in mind: Make sure your printer gives you a quality finish, keep your design and fonts simple, and have someone proof read your work before you make the official copies.

Computer templates

A simple search of the Internet will provide you with endless templates that will help you create a beautiful and unique wedding invitation. Websites, like www.microsoftoffice.com, will give you tons of great design ideas for your invitations and the templates even come with matching envelopes that you can print on your own printer as well. If you have a high-end printer, or know someone else who does, your invitations can look just as beautiful as the invitations created by a professional print shop for a tiny fraction of the price. Purchase some simple high-quality paper (as mentioned before, check out discount stores, craft stores, and business supply stores) and set aside a couple of hours to create your invitations and you're ready to go.

World Wide Web

Want a 100% free alternative to the traditional paper wedding invitation? Save a tree and the trip to the post office by using an email invitation website, like www.evite.com. There you can send out all of your invitations for free, even customize and design them yourself, people will RSVP by email, and you've cut the invitation budget down to nothing. As an added bonus, you're likely to get your replies much faster and can therefore adjust your guest list if needed.

I know to some people this may seem cheap, tacky, and not nearly formal enough for a wedding. Sometimes that's true but for some wedding themes, it's not. If you're having a small destination wedding (like Las Vegas, Mexico, or a cruise ship ceremony), and you know that only about ten people will be at the ceremony, send out an invitation by email. Or, if your budget simply can't handle another expense, send out the invites by email. It's free, it's easy, and it's good for the environment.

What your invitations should include:

- o   Names of the bride's parents

- o   Names of the bride and groom

- o Names of the groom's parents

- o Day, date, and time of wedding

- o Place of the wedding

- o Location of the reception

- o RSVP instructions

And while you're on the computer...

Use some of these other ideas to be creative with fancy paper and your computer. They'll add a personal touch but also give your wedding that special occasion feel.

Keep in mind, with every do-it-yourself project you add to your list comes another thing that is going to take up some time. Budget your time as well as your money and always ask for help when you need it.

Wedding programs

Whenever I go to a wedding ceremony, I look for the programs so that I know who's in the wedding, how long the ceremony will last, and other fun details that I might wonder about and wouldn't know without the program. However, I don't notice the quality of paper or the color of ribbon.

Guests appreciate knowing the order of the ceremony and the names of all the participants in your wedding. Even during small weddings where everyone is likely to know everyone else, it's a nice memento and a special touch for a formal occasion. Plus, your in-laws may not remember the name of your uncle who will be doing one of the readings or your parents might not remember the name of one of the groomsmen. In any case, it's a nice way to make a special occasion special.

What to include on your wedding program

Order of wedding

- o Prelude (with names of songs)

- o Processional song (with name of song)

- o Names of the readings

- o Declaration of intent

- o Exchange of vows

- o Exchange of rings

- o Names of other ceremony songs

- o Blessings

- o Recessional

Participants

- o Officiant

- o Parents of bride

- o Parents of groom

- o Maid/Matron of Honor

- Bridesmaids

- Groomsmen

- Ushers (if necessary)

- Readers

- Musicians and Soloists

- Photographer

- Personal attendant

- Flower girl (if necessary)

- Ring bearer (if necessary)

Other Information (optional)

- Couple's new address

- Honeymoon plans

- Thank you message

Again, use your computer templates to help you find a design you like. The template will guide you through the process. Just write down in the note space at the back of the book the people you think will be participating in the ceremony and then insert their names into the template and you'll have your wedding program ready in no time.

And remember, with a small wedding, you'll save money on the paper because you'll only need to make about fifty copies.

Couple profile

This is just a fun way to say a little bit about the bride and groom, how they met, where they plan to honeymoon, their future address, etcetera. You can print out a few and place them on the tables at your reception. Maybe add some wedding trivia or a crossword puzzle with facts about the family or couple. Some people might know you really well but have only hung out with your partner once or twice. It helps later in the night if they know a little more information about both of you so that conversations are a little easier to make both with you and with other guests. Inexpensive details add a nice touch to the ceremony and reception and make the event seem more formal even if you're on a fixed budget.

Dinner menu

If you're worried about the atmosphere of your dinner reception feeling less than proper, create some dinner menus. Put the menus in frames you already have or can borrow (silver frames would be elegant) and have them on all of the tables at the reception. Or print them out individually and lay them in front of each of the place settings (you can print them small, four should fit onto an 8 ½" by 11" sheet of paper). Use the same font as your invitations and programs to have a stylish and consistent look. Guests will certainly feel as if they are truly attending a special event and it's an easy and inexpensive way to make your dinner reception a more formal experience.

THE DRESS

I was dress shopping with my best friend and I saw the dress I wanted. It was gorgeous! It was also $600. I put it on hold and went home to check the Internet. There was the same dress on EBay for $80. I couldn't believe it! When I got it in the mail, I took it to get altered and pressed and on the big day it looked perfect.

Last time I checked EBay, there were approximately 800 wedding dresses for sale and some of the most gorgeous dresses I've ever seen were being sold for less than $30. No kidding, wedding dresses from EBay can be a huge bargain. Of course, use a respected buyer, make sure you always have the option to return it if you need to, and give yourself enough time to have it shipped, altered, and cleaned before your wedding day. Maybe you feel uncomfortable buying a dress online but what's more uncomfortable: paying $700 for a dress you'll wear once or paying $45 for a dress you'll wear once?

Keep an open mind because it's vital when trying to save money on something as important as your wedding day. There are so many deals on EBay; some sellers even throw in the accessories so your entire ensemble could show up on your doorstep in just a few days. You could look like a million bucks for less than the cost of a new winter coat. Shop around and check the website list in the back of the book for more places on the Internet where you can find great deals.

However, EBay is not your only option for saving hundreds of dollars on a gorgeous dress. There are other great websites that offer wedding dresses and at unbelievable prices. After doing a quick search for "discount wedding dresses" or "cheap wedding dresses", I got so many results that I had to stop looking. Most of the online stores had return options, shipping specials, and bonus gifts that came with a dress purchase. The "online" stigma of bridal dress shopping needs to be extinguished. If you throw away this option because it seems too risky, you are likely throwing away an opportunity to have a gorgeous dress for a small price. *That's* risky.

Take a look at some of these other great money saving ideas:

Something borrowed...

You know the old saying that starts with "Something borrowed something blue..." Well, why does the "something borrowed" have to be just a bracelet or a pair of earrings? Can it not be the dress itself? Truth be told, most brides would be flattered to hear that you loved their dress so much that you want to borrow it for your own wedding. As long as she is okay with you making any needed alterations and she trusts you to return it cleaned, why in the world would you not think to use a friend's or relative's wedding dress? My guess is she bought something stunning and with a hem here and tuck there, that stunning dress would be able to enjoy another celebration instead of being condemned to life in a storage closet. My wedding dress is in my closet next to the shoes

I never wore again by the jewelry I wore just that one time stashed by the veil that will never see another social outing (by the way, I purchased that veil from EBay for ten bucks and it looked exactly like the one I wanted at the bridal shop that was priced at $200).

She's Sew Self-Sufficient

Pardon the pun, but if you think you can make the dress yourself, go for it! Lots of cities offer community education classes that teach sewing for beginners and sometimes sewing classes that cater to special occasion sewing needs (like making your own wedding dress). Sign up for one of these classes and you'll not only save lots of money on your dress, you'll have the teacher and people around you who can offer advice on how to make the dress look and fit just right. All you'll need to pay for is the material and the cost of the class. It will also make the dress that much more special and unique.

Alternative Wedding Gowns

Just because you're shopping for a wedding gown doesn't mean that it has to be labeled a wedding gown. Many brides look at prom dresses (especially prom dresses that have been marked down considerably after prom season has passed). Prom dresses come in white, can be very formal, are elegant special event dresses, and are significantly cheaper than wedding gowns. Add a veil, the right jewelry, and a bouquet of flowers, and you've turned a prom dress into a gorgeous wedding gown.

Other types of dresses that can be converted into a wedding dress: Sundresses, white bridesmaid dresses, white suits, and evening gowns (these don't necessarily have to be white either!)

Look for different places to shop too. Thrift stores, consignment shops, and specialty bridal shops usually carry bridal gowns that can be bought cheap and then altered to the look you desire. Just because the dress comes with huge shoulder pads, doesn't mean that you can't have a tailor cut them out and the sleeves redone to give you a more contemporary look.

The idea is to think beyond what is traditional and conventional. If you can do that, you can save yourself hundreds of dollars and still have the wedding you want with the dress you've dreamed of.

Mini-budget check:

Dress	$
Veil	$
Shoes	$
Jewelry	$
TOTAL →	$

LET'S EAT!

The most stressful thing about planning my wedding was planning the meal at the reception. How was I going to feed all of those people for $200?

The food at a wedding reception can easily add up to the biggest expense and it seems ridiculous when you think about how many wonderful meals you've had that were twice as good as the rubbery chicken you had at your cousin's wedding. By the way, that rubbery chicken meal probably cost her $50 per plate.

Now, well-intended folks will try and tell you that a buffet dinner or an autumn wedding will save you big bucks. People also say that serving a salad would be cheaper than a soup or that chicken is less expensive than beef. But, no matter how you negotiate with your caterer, you're likely to end up with an outrageous bill and it doesn't seem right. Buffet or sit-down meal, chicken or beef, you're likely to still see a bill that can easily take you into the thousands.

It's completely understandable that you would want to have a beautiful and formal dinner after one of the biggest moments in your life. Sitting around with family and friends and celebrating the moment is exactly what a reception should be. However, spending thousands of dollars on a dinner for everyone is definitely *not* a requirement and you should never ever feel as if it is something that is expected of you.

This is a day to celebrate the union of you and your partner, so *you* should decide all of the what's, when's, and where's. You decide the menu, the party, the agenda, and the cost. Don't let tradition or "what everyone else is doing" dictate what you and your partner do. You'll likely be surprised at the number of people that say they really enjoyed going to a wedding where things were done a bit different. Just about everyone I know gets married at a church, has the photographer take all of their pictures, a limo drives them to the reception, drinks and dinner are served, a dance follows, and at the end of the night they've had a beautiful wedding but have been stressed and exhausted from the day (and of course, broke). In fact, most weddings I've attended, I'm lucky to even have a conversation with the bride or groom. They're usually running around trying to accommodate the two hundred guests they've invited or they have track down the photographer or they need to find a bridesmaid because a button fell of the back of their dress, or their mother needs them to come and meet their father's new business client, etc. There's so much chaos and with that chaos usually comes expense.

These weddings are wonderful and elegant and everything these brides and grooms thought they always wanted, but ask them later if they would change anything and I'd be willing to guess that quite a few of them would say they would have enjoyed something simpler. Why not try something different with your wedding? Let's be creative and find some ways to cut costs without sacrificing everything that the day is meant to be: a celebration of the start of new life as a married couple.

Mini-budget Check:

Food Budget ($ amount per guest)	Number of guests
$	
TOTAL →	$

Here are some ideas of how you can have fabulous food and keep the cost to a minimum. You can make these ideas special by adding your own personal touches. If we're talking about a $500 total wedding budget, we've got to get creative, especially with the big budget-buster items like food.

Time of Day

First of all, let's not plan on a meal time for your reception. If you schedule a wedding for 5:00 pm and the reception immediately follows the ceremony, people are going to be hungry for dinner when they arrive at your party. Why not push the ceremony back to 7:00pm and serve appetizers at the reception? Your guests will have likely had something to eat before the party and won't be starving for a full meal at 7:30pm. And remember what's really important; is it you feeding a hundred friends and relatives a three course meal or sharing your day with those you love the most?

If most of your guests are adults, which is likely, an evening affair is a hip and sophisticated atmosphere where your guests can have fun wearing new cocktail dress or an excuse to break out a neck tie. They'll enjoy their night out to help you celebrate your big day and I'll bet they won't care one bit about a huge meal. Even if there are going to be children at your reception, they tend to have small appetites and a large plate of food would likely be half-eaten by your younger guests. Also, consider the fact that they may not like to eat what adults like to eat so maybe a special tray of small peanut butter and jelly sandwiches or chicken nuggets with cubes of cheese would be an easier, more popular, and cheaper alternative for the kids.

Labels

Sometimes placing an order for a wedding reception automatically raises the price of the food. You'd be shocked to find out that the exact same order would have probably cost less if you hadn't mentioned it was for a wedding. Let's use the example of wedding cake. If you order five sheets of white cake, it might cost you a hundred dollars. Now, call the same bakery and order that same amount of cake (undecorated) and say it's for your wedding reception. Notice the difference in price. Just say you're having a party or a family reunion. Let's be real, you *are* having a party and a family reunion, just don't tell the bakery or caterer that you'll also be exchanging wedding vows and it could save you some bucks.

Hors d'oeuvres

Why serve a full meal when appetizers or hors d'oeuvres will more than likely get the job done. You can save oodles of money by serving appetizers because you save the cost of those little details that can kill you on a formal sit-down meal. You will need less servers, there won't be place settings, you'll need to rent less tables, chairs, tablecloths, stemware, etc. Plus, with less tables comes the added savings of less centerpieces and less clean up later.

Now, if you're going to have your reception at a restaurant, they will charge you their prices, and you might not save much money at all. If you have your reception at a place where you control costs (such as a friend's house, a park, or a church banquet hall) you will save even more money. You will have to find your own servers, someone to make the food and you'll need to determine the menu. While this may sound like a big headache, you'll probably find that relatives and friends would love to help. Think about people you know: a cousin, neighbor, coworker, your sister's friend, etc. Spend a few afternoons looking through cook books and recipe websites and you'll find tons of great ideas for affordable and delicious appetizers and hors d'oeuvres. The benefit of appetizers is that they are usually easy to assemble, transport, and they fill up a table with what appears to be a ton of food. Think about how many appetizers you'll need per person and you've got an idea on how much you'll have to spend.

And don't forget that you can always jazz something up with presentation. If your servers are all dressed in black and they serve your appetizers on borrowed silver platters, your reception will look and feel just as beautiful as a reception hall from an uptown hotel. Just don't forget to ask a few people to help clean up when the evening is over. Remember, you don't want to be the one cleaning up after your own wedding so when people say, "Is there anything I can help with?" You say, "Yes! Would you mind helping me find some people to clean up after the reception?"

There are details like this that I didn't think of when I got married and I felt so guilty at the end of the night watching my tired family clean up all of the mess in the reception hall. Put it on the list and you'll be prepared.

Does it have to be a dinner?

Sometimes we get so wrapped up in a certain time of day that we close ourselves off to other ideas that are sometimes more affordable. What about a morning ceremony in a local park or city garden followed by a brunch at your home or a friend's home? You can serve bagels and cream cheese, fresh fruit, coffee, mimosas, and pastries. To make it even more festive, spend a little bit more of your budget on a grand wedding cake. You'll save money too by making that the main centerpiece. Add some fresh flowers, borrowed antique candlesticks, some classical or jazz music playing lightly in the background and you've got a one very elegant reception.

If the weather is warm enough, people can gather outside or inside and fresh fruit and flowers won't be hard to come by. You can borrow some outdoor furniture and spread out blankets so people will feel comfortable as they visit with each other outside. If it's a cooler time of year, serve hot chocolate and use greenery from your Christmas decoration stash to make the room feel warm and cozy. Lots of candles and fire in the fireplace will make people feel relaxed and that will in turn make you and your spouse feel relaxed too.

What's really nice about doing a ceremony early in the day is that you and your husband or wife will have most of the day for yourselves. You can either keep the party going by opening the gifts after people have eaten or you can duck out of the party by early afternoon and get a head start on your honeymoon. If you choose the latter, you and your partner could be relaxing on a beach that very evening drinking wine with your feet in the sand and reliving one of the best days of your life.

Does your sweetie have a sweet tooth?

Why not do just desserts? It's everyone's favorite part of the meal and your guests would have a great time picking their favorite treats from a dessert buffet. Pick three or four finger food desserts (brownies, chocolates, tarts, peanut brittle, fudge, etc.) then some larger treats (pies, soufflés, etc.) and then of course the main attraction dessert: your wedding cake. Serve the treats with coffee, wine, tea, and pitchers of water with lemon slices. Have your dessert buffet set up at a table with borrowed silver and glass platters, some lit candles, a few vases of fresh flowers, and some light music playing under the table, behind the tablecloth.

You still will need a few people to help make sure the platters and serving trays are full and guests can find what they need (you don't want them following you around all night telling you you're out of napkins, asking you for whipped cream, or reminding you to make more coffee).

And of course, scattered all around the room, should be little bowls of chocolates, mints, and hard candies. Desserts are usually cheaper to make, easier to make, can be easily made in advance, and (depending on what you make) they don't need to be served hot or be reheated. Plus they are delicious and think of the reaction you'll get from your guests when you reveal a big table full of wonderful treats. They'll never forget *your* wedding!

Make planning your wedding a party all by itself

I hadn't seen my best friends in weeks because of all the wedding preparations so one night I called them all up and invited them over for drinks and centerpiece assembly. It was great! We laughed, caught up with each other, and got a lot done.

I planned my entire wedding in three months which to most brides seems almost impossible. It actually went fairly smoothly although all decisions had to be made quickly and all tasks had to be done immediately. That is very hard to do if you don't have help. One night I was at my parent's house and was about to start stuffing, addressing, and stamping about 250 invitations all by myself. My mom sat down to help and then some family friends called to see if we were up for a visit. We said sure, just bring a pen. So we all sat around the dining room table and had a great time catching up while we stuffed, addressed, and stamped envelopes.

I had a lot of fun that night and will cherish that memory for years to come. It was just the enjoyment of good friends helping each other accomplish a task. I think they felt pretty good about it too because they felt like they were really helping and making life a little easier for a friend.

People want to help you, it's in their nature. If your aunt knows that you are in need of someone to make your wedding cake and she's got a talent for baking, she would probably love the chance to help you. She's probably just waiting for you to ask. When the ceremony arrives and everyone gathers at the reception, those who helped you will feel a sense of pride that they were able to be there for you when you needed them.

So don't do this alone! If someone asks you if they can help, give them something to do. Refer to your to-do list.

Eating: It's not just for receptions anymore

I was a bridesmaid in my cousin's wedding and by the time I had attended the engagement party, the bridal shower, the bachelorette party, and the rehearsal dinner, I barely had enough energy or money for the wedding.

Keep in mind the cost of the entire wedding celebration. Forget the dress, the photographer, the limo, and the flowers. The real expense of weddings comes from the "little" details you don't take into account. They add up so fast that before you know it those shoes you bought for fifty bucks here and that stationary you bought for thirty bucks there add up to "where did the money go?"

One of those kinds of expenses comes from get-togethers like rehearsal dinners or groom's dinners. Family and close friends gather shortly before the wedding, usually the night before, and have dinner and drinks. Since it's another one of those events that people treat as a formality of the wedding celebration, the host usually picks up the tab for everyone's dinner and drinks. This is like paying for two wedding receptions. We're already packing all of our creative ideas into keeping costs low for the actual wedding reception, now someone needs to figure out how to pay for the food and entertainment for a rehearsal party?

Let's stop being insane about these parties. First of all, your friends and family are there to see you. They are there to help you celebrate, to visit with each other, to enjoy the good time and memory-making atmosphere that goes along with weddings and time spent with loved ones. Don't make these gatherings anything more than that. Sure, if you have a couple hundred thousand dollars to throw at a party, do it up big. But most of us bask in the simple pleasures of having those we love most in the world around us to celebrate the good things in life. So keep things simple. Have your family and close friends bring over a special dessert or a family recipe or some gourmet coffee. Everyone fills the table with their favorite foods, grabs a plate, and enjoys the moment.

Take the evening to thank everyone for sharing these days with you and especially point out those who have helped you plan for the day. Take lots of pictures, share stories, relax with your soon-to-be husband/wife, and get ready for your big day. Don't worry about fancy tablecloths or centerpieces and if you do want to use these things, just use what you have or what you can borrow. Skip the catered food and the elaborate place settings. Make simple hors d'oeuvres, have your friends and family bring something, turn on the radio for some mood music, and just take pleasure in each other's company. Don't forget to thank your future wife or husband, they've been working hard too!

Set a limit

Right now, while you're in the brain-storming stage of the wedding plans, set a food limit. And don't be vague about it either, pick a per person number of dollars you want to spend on food. It's best to think of the budget on a per person basis because it helps you keep your guest list short. We're not trying to exclude important people in your life from a very important day in your life; we're trying to achieve the most elegant wedding possible for the most affordable price we can get.

Therefore, thinking of how much it will cost if you decide to invite your lunch buddies from the office will make you think of how badly they really need to be there. If they're good friends inside and outside of the office, if they're close friends, if they're people you need to have there to make the day special, then spending the extra money would be worth it. If, however, you've only been at the company for six months or you only just started getting to know them or if they're simply just your work buddies, cut them from the list. Again, nothing says you can't get together a month or so after the wedding and buy everyone a drink at happy hour while you look through the wedding photos. You can still celebrate the big day and keep the guest list short at the same time.

Let's visualize a real number, a real amount of money that we want to spend on each person for food and drinks. If you figure one bottle of wine for every two people and five appetizers per person and everyone eats one piece of wedding cake, you would probably see a budget of five dollars per person. Now if you invite fifty people, that adds up to $250 for the food and drinks at your reception alone. That leaves just $250 left over for your dress, pictures, flowers, invitations and stamps, shoes, jewelry, film, rings, new shirt for the groom, etc. You could still make it within the $500 budget (if you follow the other tricks in this book of course) but let's say you wanted to add those four lunch buddies from work to your guest list. That's twenty more dollars added on to your food budget and if you invite them, are you then obligated to invite your boss? What if they all want to bring a guest? Are you then prepared to add fifty more dollars onto your food budget?

These are things you need to think about when you're planning out not just your guest list, but your budget as well. So sit down with your partner and think of a dollar amount that you're willing to spend on the food and drinks for the reception. Then take that number and figure out how much money it will be per person based on the number of people on your guest list. Now get creative and stick within that budget. Maybe that means you pick a more affordable bottle of wine to serve. Maybe you make a punch with wine coolers and soda instead of serving bottles of wine. Maybe you serve a less expensive hors d'oeuvre. When you set a goal that's important to you, you'll work hard and think hard in order to achieve it.

LET'S DECORATE!

I looked through tons of bridal magazines and decorating books and tried to find themes that would make our reception room warm, elegant, and happy. When I picked the look I wanted, I wrote down every detail and then found a way to pay as little as possible for it.

This is the fun stuff. At least for me and most of my female friends who are planning a wedding and reception, this is the part of the planning that is the most fun. Here, is where your creativity can shine and where the elegance and uniqueness of the day will stand out. But this book is all about saving you money and how to keep your wedding budget at $500 or less. So creativity is simply a must, especially when it comes to the décor where your heart might say spend but your head should say save.

Albert Einstein said, "The secret to creativity is knowing how to hide your sources." Does everyone at your party need to know what your decorating budget was? Do they need to know that the beautiful centerpieces were free and made out of things you found at the park or your grandmother's farm? Does everyone need to know the cost of the flowers or the candles? Of course the answer is a strong, "no!"

Be resourceful and look at the things around you, especially the things that are free. For instance, small tree branches placed in pots with greenery make the perfect place to hang glass ornaments or family pictures and the branches are free and the pictures or ornaments you already have or can borrow so without spending a dime, we have an idea for a centerpiece. For extra pizzazz, spray paint the branches a brilliant white or a shiny silver and buy some ribbon to make it look a bit more formal. Here are some more ideas:

Beautiful centerpieces that are free or almost free

• How much does a bag of tea lights cost? About five bucks and they'll burn for approximately four hours. Borrow an assortment of small glass vases, add greenery around the outside of the vases, drop a few tea lights into each vase, apply lighted match to wick and you have a warm, elegant, and inexpensive centerpiece.

• At a craft or discount store, you can purchase packs of pillar candles for around ten dollars. Buy two packs, borrow some silver or glass serving trays, put the candles on the trays, put the trays on the tables, and you have centerpieces.

• Don't buy flowers for each table, buy three or four roses and pluck the petals from each one. Scatter the petals on the tables. A pack of synthetic rose petals is just as pretty and even more affordable (about three dollars a bag at a craft store), plus you'll get twice as many for half of the cost.

• I'm guessing your friends and family has some beautiful floral arrangements or plants in their home. Could they share them with you for the evening?

• Borrow family pictures from your parents and relatives, especially old pictures of your parents and especially any pictures that your friends and family might have of you and your partner. Put them in frames you have or can borrow and place them on all of the tables.

• Just about every adult relative I know has a beautiful crystal bowl or vase that they got as a wedding gift and hardly ever use. Ask them if you could borrow it for the evening. Not only is it attractive, it's something borrowed from another family wedding celebration and that is something just as special. Now what will you put in it? Flowers, plants, or potpourri will work just fine and are very affordable, if not free.

• A dozen roses at a grocery store will cost around twenty dollars. Buy a dozen and borrow twelve small glass vases. Put one rose in each vase and put one vase on each table. Better yet, let's reuse what we have. If you're walking down the aisle with arrangement of flowers, use those flowers to put in each of the vases. At least use your bouquet somewhere at the reception as a decoration, otherwise, you'll just have to carry it around or your bridesmaid will have to find a place for it and that can be very annoying.

• What's great about Christmas decorations? The lights, the greenery, the beautiful glass ornaments, the rich colors... or is it the fact that they are beautiful decorations that almost everyone has sitting in a box somewhere in a basement and could be used at your wedding reception? Aw, I think that's it. Place simple holiday greenery around white pillar candles, use white tree lights around the baseboard of the reception room or wrapped around the staircase, take the red velvet tablecloths and silver napkin holders and use them at your tables. These are things you can borrow from your family when they ask, "Is there anything I can do to help?"

• Make the food your centerpiece. This might be the best idea of all because it blends style with purpose. Borrow silver or glass platters and have an arrangement of hors d'oeuvres, a bottle of wine, and some candles on each table. You can also have the plates and napkins stacked and the glasses out on each table so all your guests have to do is find a seat and enjoy the food and company.

• Borrow, borrow, and borrow some more. I'm sure by now you have noticed; borrowing is one of the major themes of this book. Don't feel weird about asking someone to borrow something, most people are flattered that you like something they have enough to want to borrow it. You're not freeloading off someone, you're giving someone the chance to help you and most people want to help and like to help. Give them the chance. Think of some of your friends that have gotten married recently. What did they use for their centerpieces? One of my best friends let me borrow the 50 glass vases she bought for her wedding to use as centerpieces at my wedding. She also let me borrow a beautiful silver candleholder. She was more than happy to help me and even volunteered them to me before I ever thought to ask. They were just sitting in boxes in her parent's garage and she was thankful that they would get some use again.

It's not about using people for things that they have that you want, it's about asking people for help. If they say no, be understanding and respectful and then think of some other way to get what you need.

Skip the banquet halls, hotels, and ballrooms

Yes, these places can be downright beautiful. They can be lovely, elegant, and glamorous. They can also be wildly expensive. When my husband and I got married, the hotel ballroom we rented cost us over five hundred dollars for just the use of the space. Then, because we were using their ballroom, we also had to use their caterer, bartender, and liquor. The cost was unbelievable. They also added on these crazy fees that didn't make any sense and when all of it was said and done I felt like we had totally been scammed.

Skip looking at banquet halls, hotels, and ballrooms altogether if you want to stay within your budget. Not only will you save money by forgetting about these venues, you will have the freedom to do more with the space you have. The money you save from renting their space and buying their food is tremendous, plus you won't have hotel rules or caterer schedules to worry about.

Find a willing friend or relative with a large home or area for your guests to be comfortable and ask them for their help. Most people would be flattered that you thought their home was suitable for a wedding reception. Plus now you have the freedom to decorate in a more intimate setting.

With our large hotel ballroom wedding reception, we couldn't afford large centerpieces and our cake was tiny. When we had everything out on the tables and the cake was delivered, the space of the room swallowed up the centerpieces I had worked so hard on and our wedding cake looked like a cupcake. I'm sure I'm the only one it really bothered, but I remember that feeling of thinking that my hard work was all for nothing and that was just one more thing that stressed me out on my wedding day. That, and the fact that the hotel's caterers charged us a fee to cut the cake.

Give me a break.

Ask any bride that's gone the traditional route with a wedding budget and they'll tell you horror stories about the amount of extra fees that businesses tack on for weddings and receptions. The wedding business is big business so be careful at every turn to make sure you're saving as much money as you can.

Have your cake serve more than one purpose

It's tradition, it's delicious, and it can be expensive. Instead of a large three tiered wedding cake with all of the frills, make small cakes and use them as centerpieces at the tables. When the guests are finished eating, have your servers cut the cakes for your guests (you can make them all different flavors so your guests will be surprised!) and now your cake- excuse me, your cakes- have done more than decorate your tables, they've fed your guests and saved you money!

Cakes are surprisingly easy to make and order if you're not putting them in the "wedding cake" category. Here's what I'm talking about: If you go to a caterer and say, "I'm interested in buying a wedding cake" you won't see one that's less than $100. If you go to your grocer's bakery and ask for ten small white cakes with white frosting, you're going to get a much better deal. Then, the day of your wedding, have someone pick up the cakes, put them on the tables, and use some flowers (washed first please) to place on top of each cake. It's inexpensive and really beautiful.

Be resourceful

Exhaust all possibilities when it comes to saving money. Think about what you want and the look you're going for and then brainstorm the most affordable way you can get it. Let's say you're thinking of a brunch instead of an evening gathering. You won't need a bunch of candles and you probably won't need a lot hors d'oeuvres either. Concentrate on things that would make a brunch charming; like flowers, tea, classical music, and sunshine.

Straight away, let's think about those flowers. Flowers aren't cheap so we need to brainstorm some ideas. First of all, use what you have. As mentioned before, those flowers you carry down the aisle can be used again as décor for your reception. Then use a small potted plant in place of large floral bouquets. Buy your flowers the day before or of if you have time at your local floral shop or grocery store. Buy a few less expensive kinds of flowers and mix them with a few higher-priced flowers. To make it look less mismatched, buy flowers that are all one color. For instance, buy white carnations and mix them with white roses and lilies.

Apply this thinking to other things you'll need for your décor. Are you going with an evening reception and need lots of candles or candleholders? Buy a few, borrow a lot. When the day is over, you're not going to need twenty of the same candleholder or twenty half burned candles. Maybe you can buy the pillar candles and borrow all of the candleholders. Maybe mix candlesticks (a lot less expensive) with the pillar candles, some tea lights, and floating candles. Think of places where you can buy these cheap: yard sales, dollar stores, after-holiday sales, etc. Make a list of everything you'll need for the ceremony and reception decorations and find a free or almost free way to get it. You'll be surprised at your creativity and ingenuity.

LET'S PARTY!

At first, I was a little nervous about having my reception in my aunt and uncle's backyard. I mean, they have a huge backyard, but how would it look as a wedding reception? It turned out awesome! We put out several tables with tablecloths and white candles. We added a rented canopy to put the food under and put some white Christmas tree lights around it for extra pizzazz. Everyone had plenty of room to move around and dance and visit. It was a great night!

Finding a place to host your big after-ceremony bash can be fun at first. You look at all of those great movies about weddings and their elaborate décor and the fancy atmosphere and perfect locations. Wedding magazines show lovely gardens and gorgeous beaches where couples are wed in high fashion and dripping in jewelry. It makes for a nice image but an almost unattainable reality.

Who do you know can afford these things and yet are we all doomed to a wedding reception in a pool hall because we lack the million dollar wedding budget?

The answer is of course, absolutely not and listed below (all within the $500 wedding budget by the way) are several charming locations for your wedding reception. Just remember the rules; be creative, ask for help, and use every single resource you have. Here are some ideas where you can have a beautiful wedding and reception for a small price.

City parks and gardens

There might be a fee associated with renting park space but it's usually less than $100. If bad weather surprises you on your wedding day, some park districts even offer a second indoor location at no extra cost. City parks and/or gardens offer much more than just a space for you to put everyone, they are beautiful, cost you almost nothing on decorations, have plenty of room for your guests, provide a built-in backdrop for your photographs, and are a unique and charming place to not just have your reception but exchange vows as well.

In fact, you'll save lots of time and money by having your ceremony and reception at the same location. You won't have to find transportation to the reception, you won't have to decorate two places, and you're guests will appreciate the convenience of just staying put. You'll need to check with your particular park district about the length of time you'll be allowed to stay, if alcoholic beverages are allowed on the site, and what the particular rules are for the park you choose to use.

Remember the perks too of having control over the location of your reception. You choose the food, who makes it, how much it costs, how it will be served, etcetera. No weird fees that caterers and hotels are likely to charge you. You're in charge of the tables, chairs, place settings, décor, and drinks, but you'll still be saving *thousands* of dollars.

Overall, this is a beautiful and much more special alternative to a hotel ballroom or banquet hall. It's a very charismatic location that you and your guests will really enjoy. A place where you can feel comfortable but still has the feeling that it's a special occasion and depending on the location, you'll have a beautiful place to take pictures!

The home of a close friend or family member

If one of your relatives, close friends, or even you have the space and atmosphere for a special event like a wedding reception- seriously consider using it. Like with the city park or garden, you are in control of the reception space and will save tons of money by choosing the food and forgoing the fees associated with hotels, caterers, ballrooms, etc. Again, try and get the most bang for your buck by having the ceremony at the same place as your reception as well. If you feel weird about asking someone to use their home for such a big occasion, think about what you can offer them in exchange.

For instance, if you are asking your aunt with the lovely lake home if she'd be willing to let you have the reception there, enlist a large group of friends to do the set up and clean up afterwards. You could also offer money, I know we're trying to save wherever possible but even spending $100 on a location is a *huge* savings compared to the overly formal and traditional hotel ballroom. Plus, she'll probably be flattered and willing to help however she can.

I also know of a couple who lived in a beautiful apartment on a lake and the apartment complex featured a "party room." It was gorgeous with a gas fireplace, classic décor, a kitchen area, and a breathtaking view with plenty of indoor and outdoor space. The fee associated with renting the room was actually a deposit which meant that if everything was cleaned and put back after the party, that money went towards the couple's rent for the next month.

In major cities there are many office buildings that have beautiful gathering spaces that are often on lakes or close to parks. I went to a wedding once that was *way* over $500 and the reception was held in an office building. Believe it or not, it was gorgeous.

You've got to think of all of these possibilities and exhaust all ideas and resources when trying to save money. You will be surprised at the gorgeous reception you could have for such a small price if you're willing to brainstorm some ideas.

Dinner at the church

If you are like me and your religion requires you to be married in a church, then exchanging your vows at a park or a friend's home isn't a possibility. However, who says you can't move the party to the church? Most churches offer a reception room or dining hall because this is where a lot of gathering takes place for after-church meetings, coffee and donuts, funeral receptions, church board meetings, etc. They often have a kitchen are a blank canvas just waiting for you to decorate.

Another perk is that it will probably cost you next to nothing to rent. You will probably have the option to use church volunteers to help you serve or prepare the meal (you will need to offer them some money though since they are not serving at an actual church function, still your savings will be tremendous). You will also probably have plenty of time to decorate, even the morning of, just show up a little earlier to add your last minute touches. For those in smaller communities, this is a huge option for you. Your community might not offer several different banquet halls or ballrooms so if there is one close by, it has no incentive to be competitive with its pricing since it's the only game in town. After the dinner, move the dancing and music to a friend's home and enjoy cocktails and jazz music with your guests. Don't forget about the convenience too of just moving to another room after the ceremony. You can take a few minutes somewhere private to enjoy a post-ceremony moment with your new husband/wife and then go down the hall to the dinner room to be with friends and family. There's no reception line or a limo driver who doesn't show up (that happened to my sister) or keeping track of your bridesmaids. Everything is all together and ready for you to enjoy.

Another perk about keeping it at the church for awhile is that a lot of churches have beautiful gardens on their property. This presents a wonderful opportunity to get some formal pictures in. Even if there isn't a place outside to take pictures, churches are beautiful inside as well. My husband and I got married in the winter and didn't get any outdoor pictures. All of ours were in the church and they turned out great.

Keep this in mind as well, if you are from a large family or your partner is and you can't seem to trim your guest list down to fifty or less, this is a great option for you. Church reception halls usually hold quite a few people, and the money you've saved on the location can be put into feeding more people. After the reception, you can still plan on a small cocktail party at a friend's or family member's home and any guests with children might find this easier too. They can visit with everyone at the dinner with their kids and then bring them home afterwards to a babysitter so they can enjoy the cocktail party with you.

Make Reservations

Think about how many people are on your guest list. If you've really stuck to the 50 or less plan, what about making reservations at one of your favorite nice restaurants that has a party room for large groups? You can look at the menu before hand and decide what works in your budget. Order plates of appetizers and tell the server that each guest gets one drink on the bride and groom. You can even specify the drink so that you can stick to your budget and your server won't be swamped with fifty different drink orders. Set aside five or six bottles of wine and have the server ask each guest if they'd like a glass of wine or a soda. Be upfront with your budget and the amount you're willing to spend.

There are lots of advantages with this plan. First, you will have a venue that will require less (if any) decorating, less borrowing of things like plates and tablecloths, and you won't have to find someone to help clean up or wash dishes. Your servers will be dressed up, professional, and eager to help.

Second, you will likely get a discount for ordering in advance. If you tell the restaurant, we want to spend $300 here and our guests will likely be ordering more drinks and possibly food on their own. Can we get a couple of free appetizers for our business? If it's a newer restaurant, stress the fact that they will be exposing their restaurant to a group of new customers who will spread their name around town. They will likely go along with it, especially if you order ahead of time. Just remember, that it will be *very* important to tip well so make sure that you budget at least 20% of what you plan to spend on dinner to go to your server.

Third, if you pick a place that's got other amenities like live music or a DJ you are getting even more for your money. Lots of places feature these entertainment extras on certain nights of the week anyway. Some places, especially those that have recently opened for business, will be happy to have the crowd. Ask if they'll play a few requests for you and you're getting a great deal on entertainment and music. You may want to save some bucks to tip the band or DJ well, especially if you're requesting some special songs for your first dance or a father/daughter dance. Either way, you are getting a great deal on what will likely be a very fun reception. And if you're getting a good deal on things that you would otherwise be paying for separately than you might be able to spend more money on something like pictures or your dress.

Mostly remember that it's who is with you, not necessarily where you are, that will make the night a success. You're going to be with your new wife/husband, your closest friends and family members and making memories that will last a lifetime. Keep an open mind about where your party will be held and you will very likely walk away with a great deal and a fun venue.

SAY CHEESE!

This was the one expense I was worried I wouldn't be able to afford and the one thing I really wanted at the end of the day.

Wedding photographers can be fabulous. They can be very creative with their portrait ideas, they know the right lighting to use, and they can get the flower girl to smile during the big group shot. And if we had more than a $500 budget, I'd say find the one you want and pay whatever they ask because pictures of big moments in your life are priceless and your wedding photographs will be cherished for generations.

However, we don't have an endless budget. We have $500 for the whole thing. But do *not* get discouraged. This is when you need to roll up your sleeves, gather the troops, and get creative. We're going to get you some awesome wedding pictures and still stay within the budget.

Everyone knows someone who takes great pictures

Have you ever had someone show you their vacation pictures and you thought, "Wow, this person really knows how to use a camera." Call that person and make sure they're at your wedding. Did your uncle just get a cool new digital camera? Make sure he's there with that new camera. Did your sister take photography classes in college? She needs to bring her camera too.

Here's my point: Lots of people will be bringing their camera to a wedding, just make sure that the people you know with a real eye for photography are getting the shots you really want. You want them all there taking pictures, a lot of pictures, *tons* of pictures (that's the great thing about digital cameras). When the day is finally over, have them put all of the pictures on a CD for you. You and your spouse can look over the pictures, find your favorites, and either print them out right away or later when you've got more money. One of many perks to having digital photographs is that you can embellish the pictures anyway you want. Crop a picture, make it black and white, blow it up, add more or less contrast, make pictures brighter or darker, whatever you want you can do it on your own and save thousands of dollars.

Check out some local computer classes and software to get some ideas on how to make qualities touches to your photographs.

The talented amateur photographers you've enlisted for help will likely know how much lighting they'll need, they'll take pictures at the right angles, and you won't end up with pictures featuring someone's thumb. Plus, they'll be thrilled you asked and it could inspire them to take it on as a part-time job in which case they could put you down as a reference!

Make a list

Know exactly what pictures you want because it will be up to you to make sure you get them. Especially if you're enlisting the help of people who do not do this as a full-time career, you're going to need to know what pictures you want and when. *See the list at the end of this book for inspiration.*

Find a rookie

In addition to the amateur photographers that you'll have at your wedding, find a rookie. When I say rookie, I mean someone studying photography in college. Post a flyer at local universities and community colleges stating something like this: *Photographer Needed for Wedding! Pay is $50 for one hour and the negatives. Call this number if you're interested...* Use them only for the ceremony and the big shots from the above list. You'll need them only for about an hour so $50 will be plenty (budget another ten bucks if you want them to be there extra twenty minutes). Tell them if you like their work, they can use you as a reference. Also, just get the negatives from them. If you want to spend a bit more and have them make a few prints for you, budget for that, but really you just want the negatives. When you've got the money for prints later, take them to a photographer and find out how much it will cost for the prints.

If your rookie photographer can do both digital and regular photographs, that's even better. They can put everything on a CD for you and give you the negatives and you're set. It should be noted that universities and area schools are a wonderful resource in general when planning a wedding or big event. They are loaded with talented people who need real-world experience and references to put on their resumes when they are ready to graduate. Their fees are dirt cheap (if anything at all) and they are usually eager to help.

Remember, one of the rules is Be Resourceful. Think about using a student if you want cheap live music at your ceremony, some decoration tips for your reception, photographs, recipes, invitations, and more.

Try a professional

This is risky but call around a find out how much a professional would cost for just one hour, you may be surprised. I really don't recommend this because you're likely to get a big sales pitch for a picture package you simply can't afford. Or they may claim it will only be $75 and then tack on fees later that you weren't prepared for. However, you won't know unless you ask. There may be a new portrait studio in town that could use some word-of-mouth advertising. There may be a new photographer fresh out of school who could use the exposure. Make some phone calls and find out but stay strong and firm with your budget. Don't get scammed or bullied by a professional who just wants the business.

The trick to hiring either the rookie or the professional is to state the price you are willing to pay and the work they will be paid for. If they know up front that you have a specific dollar amount in mind and you're unwilling to waver on that amount (which is a good thing!) then you will save yourself having to negotiate a price or listening to a long sales pitch.

In closing, I agree that pictures are one of the most important parts of the day. They are the one thing you can keep for years and years to remind you of one of the happiest days of your life. If having a deluxe picture package is especially important to you but not in the budget, consider asking for it as a wedding gift. Maybe it's something all of the grandparents or your parents can go in on and it's definitely something they can enjoy as well.

TOP TEN SILLIEST WEDDING EXPENSES

I can't believe I spent that much money on wedding favors only to find half of them on the floor or in the garbage!

These well-intentioned details are meant to let people know they have been invited to a very special event. This isn't just a *party*, it's a wedding reception. But let's get serious about money; is all of this formality worth it? You or whoever is paying for most of your wedding will likely go into debt with all of the added expense and even if the money has been saved, wouldn't it be better spent on a down payment for a house, a honeymoon, paying off some existing debt, a new car, etc. I guarantee that the people invited to your wedding will not care one bit about the color of your invitations, personalized napkins, or how much your shoes cost.

To be honest, most of these costly details go unnoticed. At best, they serve as a conversation piece around the table during dinner. I have received wedding favors that I knew must have cost the couple a bundle but honestly, I didn't use them for anything after the night was over. What your guests care about is you and your spouse, so keep the focus on the special day and forget about the extra frills. Besides, in most cases they're pretty cheesy.

1. Party favors

You're kidding me with these things right? The purpose of these money-wasters is, I think, to commemorate the day. But can everyone just admit that most of these favors are tacky and weird? I have received as a wedding party favor a wide variety of things including a book of matches, a potted plant, a bag of candy, a small bottle of wine, a jar of wild rice, a bottle of bubbles, and a paper weight. And, as an added plus, almost all of them had either a picture or the names of the celebrated couple pasted on it. It's like my house is now a museum of wedding memorabilia collected during my twenties. Thanks but no thanks.

2. Ice sculptures and personalized napkins

Both of these extravagances do the exact same thing: cost a fortune and end up making a mess all over the floor. I don't need to see a swan made out of ice to know it's a special occasion and I certainly don't need to wipe my mouth all over a napkin that has your name printed on it in gold lettering. Save your money and the headache that undoubtedly goes along with ordering these lavish extras.

3. Over-the-top invitations

If you have never received one of these invitations, be thankful. On the outside, it appears to be a simple envelope, but on the inside is a whirlwind of paper, confetti, pictures, and information. You open the envelope only to find another envelope and when you open that envelope you're bombarded with silver wedding bell confetti, a picture of the bride and groom, another envelope, and random sheets of blank tissue paper. You spread the invitation across your kitchen table and realize with this one piece of mail you have enough inventory to start your party supply store. These multi-layered vellum nightmares (which usually come in square envelopes that require an extra postage cost) can easily rob your budget of hundreds of dollars and are completely unnecessary.

Stick to the basics, a beautiful crisp and clean font on a simple and elegant paper. Skip the pictures, ribbons, confetti, and the pre-stamped RSVP reply cards. Have people RSVP by email or telephone. It's better for your budget and the environment plus, you have instantly saved yourself $500 at least.

4. Save-the-date cards

With apologies to my sister who did use save-the-date cards, these are basically another mailing expense, paper and design expense, and a huge overall waste of money and trees. It makes about as much sense as friends calling you to tell you that in a month they plan on calling you again and inviting you to dinner.

If you're worried about people being busy on your wedding day, keep two things in mind: One, you're having a small and intimate wedding where the people invited wouldn't dream of missing your big day.

And two, if you're really worried about it, you can always send out your invitations a few weeks earlier than planned. Plus, those invited will probably be talking about it and the word will spread among your guest list without you having to fret about people not saving the date.

5. Lavish gifts for the bridesmaids, groomsmen, flower girl, ring bearer, ushers, personal attendant, minister...

Enough already; these people are honored (or should be) just to be a part of your wedding day, they don't need engraved silver key chains or designer cosmetic cases as a way for you to show your gratitude. Yes, I agree that a little something for those who went above and beyond for you on your wedding day is a wonderful thing to do (and something you should do), however, I'm always amazed at the expectations people put on themselves. Find something nice for your special people but make it something meaningful.

For instance, instead of spending $20 each on new earrings for each of your bridesmaids, why not get them each a small frame with a picture of you and her in it. How about a potted plant with a note telling her how special she is to you? Another thing to keep in mind is the number of people in your bridal party. If you we're keeping with the small and intimate affair rule, then just being invited shows those on the guest list that are someone very special to you. You will not need to have four or even three bridesmaids (unless you have some sort of sister obligation); a maid-of-honor should get the job done just fine.

6. The guest book with the feather pen, the cake knife, the candelabra

Now, these are things that actually are needed (except for that crazy feather pen) but where the wasted expense comes from is when we brides feel we need to buy all of these things or they have to look a certain way. For instance, I bought a white wedding guest book for something like $20 that maybe 8% of my guests signed. It's currently in a storage box in my garage I think. The cake knife that was for sale next to the guest book was about the same price and had a white ribbon tied around it. I thankfully passed on the knife and borrowed a beautiful silver candelabra from one of my bridesmaids (the church we were married at required we use our own candelabra for the lighting of the unity candle, which we also had to buy). We saved a bunch of money by borrowing the candelabra and using the caterer's knife to cut the cake but looking back, I wish I would have done a better job saving money on that guest book. My sister used a frame for about the same price that had a large space for the guests to sign. We had it out in the church early before the ceremony started and since those closest to her and her husband arrived first, I made sure they all signed it. It turned out really nice and is something that she could actually display in their home.

Other guest book ideas include: a leather bound journal that you could later keep on a bookshelf, a scrapbook or photo album that has space for guests to write a message, or a blank canvas (about $5 at a craft store) that guests could sign and you could later display with pictures of you and your spouse from your wedding or honeymoon.

7. Huge fancy wedding cakes

Wedding cakes are my favorite reception tradition, mostly because I like to eat cake. But they really are a fun way to celebrate and should be included in your budget. However, wedding cakes do not need to be wonders of architecture and engineering. They don't need elaborate icing or twenty roses made out of frosting.

To be sure, those cakes are lovely and delicious, and probably cost hundreds of dollars. I've seen plain white cakes that are gorgeous with fresh flowers added to the top. I've seen small lovely cakes that make a statement when guests arrive at the party but sheet cakes in the back are actually served to the guests and the guests couldn't care less.

There are ways to get around the huge expense of wedding cakes, and be sure to remember that bakeries will charge extra for a cake labeled a "wedding cake" because they know most people will just pay it. Don't be one of those people. You're way too clever for that.

8. Personalized candles, confetti, water bottles, wine bottles, and chocolates

These are just so expensive and such a hit to your budget. They are also things that go unnoticed by guests and let's admit this too: They are cheesy.

9. Expensive cake toppers

I know people who have spent $100 for collectable figurines to place on their cake or have used an elaborate rhinestone letter that celebrates their last name. Don't do it, just don't do it. It's one of those expenses that you'll regret after the wedding is over. If you're looking for something special to top your cake with, look at family heirlooms. A glass angel from your mother or a silver bell inherited from your grandmother. Use some of the flowers from your bouquet. Just please don't spend money on something to put on top of your cake. It's like the shoes you wear under your dress; even the few that notice them won't remember them.

10. Wedding cameras on the reception tables

They're about five dollars per camera (and that's a conservative number) and the idea is that the guests will take candid photos at the reception that you and your partner will enjoy later. Only what happens is you get fifty pictures with Uncle Phil's thumb in the lens and the other fifty pictures were taken without a flash. Just have everyone bring their own camera if they want to take pictures. Besides, people usually prefer to use their own camera.

I was at a wedding where the bride had these cameras on the tables (actually she spent a lot of money on each thing on this list). She was so mad when she discovered that the "photographers" using these cameras were her little cousins and nieces and nephews. She got in a fight with one of the bridesmaids and made a scene about how expensive the cameras were. This is a classic case of how just because you have more money to spend on your wedding doesn't mean it will run any smoother. In fact, by having less things to worry about (and less money to spend on the silly wedding expenses) you'll have less to stress about on your big day.

These silly wedding expenses are expenses that, in my opinion, are unnecessary but if there's something you really want from this list: go for it. Just budget and try to keep the three rules in mind.

Always remember what your top wedding priority is and really make sure every purchase is something worthwhile. And it really better be worthwhile because whatever category you add money to, you'll have to subtract money from another category.

10 WEDDINGS THAT COST $500 OR LESS

You may have read the whole book, all of the tricks and tips, and you are still skeptical about how in the world you can have a wedding and reception for $500 or less. Or maybe you picked up this book and flipped right to this section because you didn't want to waste anymore time on it if you thought it wouldn't work. I don't blame you; I would do the exact same thing. And why wouldn't you be a little skeptical? This is your wedding day! We want a beautiful wedding that is nothing less than special.

So let's go through ten real wedding ideas. These are ten real wedding themes with their budgets broken down into nice round numbers that you can use as a guide to get you going on your wedding budget. Adjust the budget to fit your needs, always making sure to add or subtract from categories to stay within the $500.

You can do this! These weddings are all unique in their own way. They are also special, charming, meaningful, and ready for you to add your personal touches to them. So start daydreaming and then start moving- your wedding day will be here soon!

Seaside Ceremony

♥

Location: If you live by the sea (or a big beautiful lake or river), you should take advantage of the free decorations. Think about a beautiful sandy ceremony at a local seaside park, on the docks, or directly on the beach with your feet in the sand.

Bride and bridal party: The bride in a white sundress with an easy hairstyle, like long curls that can twist in the breeze. The bride should wear maybe one piece of sentimental jewelry and flowers in her hair. Bridesmaids should wear something similar, maybe light yellow or green sundresses and remember, if you're on the beach, no shoes or sandals needed!

Groom and groomsmen: The groom in khaki pants and a crisp white button down shirt, sleeves rolled up and the rings in his pocket. Groomsmen should wear something similar, maybe shirts in a different color. And again, shoes or sandals are probably not needed!

Ceremony: Outdoor ceremonies are usually shorter than indoor ceremonies so think of simple seating arrangements. You can rent folding chairs for your event or if, you really want it easy, lay beach blankets in the sand and have your guests soak in the sun and relax on the beach. Flowers should be whatever is in season and bought the day before, or morning of your ceremony. Skip the florist; just have a friend or family member pick up some flowers at the local nursery. The bride will need a small but fanciful arrangement, like daisies or lilacs and the bridesmaids can stand up for their bride with just one stem of whatever the bride chooses. Forget about the boutonnieres for the groomsmen, only the groom should have one. For music, find someone who can play a few songs for you on an acoustic guitar which is perfect for the beach.

Reception: If possible, keep the party right there on the beach or in the park. Picture small tables with candles, white table cloths, a few flowers, and bottles of wine. Serve some type of finger food like petite sandwiches or a shrimp cocktail. Skip a big dinner and stick with just appetizers and wine. Pick out some reggae music and keep it playing throughout the reception.

Final thoughts: Send thank you notes to your guests on postcards that feature the beach on which you were married.

Budget		
The dress	$50	Sundress bought on sale
Groom's attire	$25	Bought white dress shirt, no tie
Accessories	$15	Necklace borrowed from friend, earrings bought new

Flowers	$30	White daisies bought day of wedding with long blades of grass, tied with simple white ribbon
Pictures	$50	Hired college student, used three friends as well, uncle taped wedding
Music	$10	Friend played acoustic guitar during ceremony, recorded music played during dinner and reception
Food and drinks	$225	Small sandwiches and shrimp cocktail were served with wine and wedding cake
Decorations	$20	Flowers from ceremony were put in vases filled with sand and shells, white candles and shells were placed on all the tables, tables had white tablecloths, chairs each had a white ribbon tied to them
Invitations	$25	Made on bride's computer
Miscellaneous	$25	Always a good idea to have a little left over for the unexpected expense

Fall Ball

♥

Location: This is best for a country location; a barn or open field where you can soak in the great outdoors. Keep in mind it might be a cool fall night so try and find a place where a bonfire would work. If you live in the city but want a wedding like this, a local park might be able to accommodate.

Bride and bridal party: The bride would look perfect in an ivory gown with a bouquet of flowers, greenery, and leaves in the colors orange, red, yellow, and brown. Make sure your attire is weather-appropriate, if it's cold, you'll need a warm wrap. Your bridesmaids should dress in a gorgeous autumn color, like maroon, emerald green, violet, chocolate, or gold.

Groom and groomsmen: A dark suit with a nice shirt in a rich color (suggestions listed above) would look very sharp on the groom. Have the groomsmen wear something similar in a complimentary color.

Ceremony: You can walk down an isle of beautiful fall leaves in their most stunning colors. You could serve hot cocoa or apple cider to the guests before the ceremony and have them bring a warm wool blanket to cuddle up with while you exchange vows. The trees and their colors will provide the backdrop for your pictures which will likely be gorgeous. If you know anyone who plays the violin, it would work beautifully with this theme, a guitar would sound lovely too.

Reception: Bob for apples, go on a hay ride, serve apple cider and pumpkin pie instead of wedding cake. For food, have something warm and hearty for guests to eat. Try large pots of chili or potato soup with homemade bread and apples. When decorating, take advantage of the beautiful foliage: Scatter colorful leaves on the table tops and use vases to hold water with floating candles. Let the nature around you do the decorating; some candles, nice tablecloths, and maybe some white Christmas lights are all you'll really need. A bonfire with some light music playing in the background would be a perfect way to close the evening.

Final thoughts: This is really a special kind of wedding with lots of opportunities to cuddle up with your new husband/wife. You'll need to plan for the weather, but with some ingenuity and helpful volunteers, you should have no problem making this a beautiful wedding.

Budget		
The dress	$80	Dress bought online, warm velvet wrap made by a friend
Groom's attire	$25	Used own suit, bought new shirt and borrowed a tie from his father

Accessories	$0	Necklace and earrings were borrowed from her mother
Flowers	$40	Bunches of evergreen taken from a friend's yard were paired with flowers bought that day in rich fall colors
Pictures	$50	Hired college student, used three friends as well, cousin taped wedding
Music	$10	Sister played the violin during ceremony, recorded music played during dinner and reception
Food and drinks	$220	Chili, homemade bread, fresh apples, hot chocolate, cider, wine and wedding cake were served
Decorations	$30	Flowers from ceremony were put in vases for reception, green, purple, and gold candles were placed on all the tables, tables had dark tablecloths, chairs each had evergreen tied to them, red Christmas lights
Invitations	$25	Made on bride's computer
Miscellaneous	$20	Just in case

Vegas Baby!

♥

Location: Las Vegas. Now, despite what you might think of Vegas weddings, they are not all cheap, cheesy, or tacky. They can be very elegant, tasteful, and still affordable. For example, you can get married at the Grand Canyon for less than $5000, but since this book is all about how to get married for $500 or less, let's look at some less expensive options.

Bride and bridal party: The great thing about being in a place where so many people elope is that you have resources not usually available to you in other locations. For instance, you can rent wedding dresses in Vegas, saving you tons of money. Better yet, find a dress during post-prom season that has been marked down significantly. A fun but pretty cocktail dress would work perfectly and then you're set for the rest of the evening. You won't have to worry about a train or a long flowing dress, just you in something simple and looking gorgeous. Also, forget about fancy jewelry or a huge headpiece, think simple and sophisticated. For bridesmaids, have them wear their best dress although keep in mind, Vegas weddings are usually very small and the bridesmaids and groomsmen (if you have any) will likely be seated instead of standing up at the altar with you and your husband.

Groom and groomsmen: No need for a tuxedo, although if he wants to rent one, there are more than enough places that can help him. But a less stressful route would be to wear a nice black suit with a fresh white shirt and a white tie.

Ceremony: The great thing about Vegas is that so many of their packages include the basics that you will need, for example flowers, photos, and music. Keep in mind that there's usually a "minister fee" that is not included in the package price and is accepted as cash only. The minister fee is usually around $50. Packages that include flowers and photos (the music is almost always included at no extra charge) usually run in the neighborhood of $300. You can obviously go bigger and spend around $700 for more photos and extras but you can also go smaller with very simple ceremonies for as little as $150.

Your biggest expense is getting to Vegas unless you live close by but Las Vegas is famous for their vacation deals and even spending a couple hundred on flights and a hotel room, you can still do your ceremony for less than $500 depending on the time you decide to travel (midweek will cost less than a weekend and a September vacation is usually less expensive than a December vacation.)

Reception: Pretty easy to plan, in fact, if it's just you and your new husband/wife then maybe not having a definite plan would be more fun. You're already in Las Vegas so the entertainment is abundant. After your ceremony, find a nice place to eat and then go to a show, play some black jack, or just relax in your hotel suite with the lights of strip twinkling in the background.

Final thoughts: Las Vegas can be a very romantic place to exchange vows, if you have any preconceived notions about tacky Vegas weddings, let them go and you could have a really beautiful and affordable wedding day.

Also, Vegas doesn't have to be a place you sneak off to. Invite family and friends, most wedding packages will accommodate small weddings at a very affordable price. For the very thrifty, you can have a private ceremony with just you and your partner and it's even more affordable if you plan something mid-week, before noon.

Budget		
The dress	$50	White prom dress bought post-prom season, on sale
Groom's attire	$50	Used own suit, bought new shirt and shoes, borrowed a tie
Accessories	$40	Earrings bought new, necklace borrowed from friend, bride bought new shoes
Flowers	$0	Package included flowers
Pictures	$20	Package came with some pictures included, extra prints were bought, and friends took more pictures

Music	$0	Package came with recorded music
Food and drinks	$250	Went out for nice dinner after the ceremony
Decorations	$0	Provided at the chapel
Invitations	$0	Sent email invitations
Miscellaneous	$70	Minister fee and marriage license

Under the Stars

♥

Location: Anywhere with a great view of the stars. A large backyard, a rooftop, even a boat on the water- just some place out in the open where the stars can be seen in all their glory.

Bride and bridal party: The bride in a simple evening dress and if the weather is cold, add a velvet or silk wrap. This is an atmosphere where a formal white bridal dress wouldn't be the best choice. You're getting married in the dark, outside, with little if any isle to walk down. A big formal wedding dress wouldn't work here so aim for something more in the prom section. And with this theme, white is optional, color might be more fun.

Groom and groomsmen: The groom in a classic black suit would be perfect and the groomsmen in formal white button down shirts with black pants. If it's cold, have them throw on the matching jackets.

Ceremony: For seating arrangements, rent or borrow folding chairs and set them up in two blocks thus forming a center isle. Arrange for white Christmas lights to be strung around any bushes or pillars and dig out the artificial green Christmas trees, keep them plain green with only white lights. Using lots of candles will also add atmosphere. This should be an extremely intimate wedding with little décor, just enough to let guests know something special is happening but not enough to take away from the real decorations, the stars above. The ceremony should be surrounded with simple lighting, just the candles, a few white Christmas lights, and of course, the stars. The bride should carry a small bouquet of flowers and find someone to serenade you with a saxophone.

Reception: A formal outdoor evening picnic is the theme here. Visualize candles on all of the tables with cake, bottles of wine, fruit, and crackers and cheese. Some jazz music in the background and your set.

Final thoughts: There's something very calm and peaceful about a clear night outside, take advantage of this and soak up the memory of your wedding. Also, music is a very inexpensive way to set the mood, especially being outside, you're also going to want to drown out any traffic or other outdoor noises. Have CD players placed all over your reception area, some suggestions: Anything by Norah Jones, Frank Sinatra, Nat King Cole, and Tony Bennett.

Budget		
The dress	$60	Prom dress bought on sale, borrowed a wrap from aunt
Groom's attire	$30	Bought white dress shirt, used own tie and suit
Accessories	$10	No necklace, bought earrings on sale

Flowers	$10	Bride walked down the aisle with single red rose, groom had rose boutonniere (flowers bought that afternoon)
Pictures	$50	Hired college student, used three friends as well, uncle taped wedding
Music	$10	Friend played the saxophone during ceremony, recorded jazz music played during dinner and reception
Food and drinks	$250	It's a late night wedding so just desserts, wine, crackers, cheese and wedding cake are served
Decorations	$30	Rose petals scattered on tables, tea light candles and silver dessert platters on all the tables, tables had white tablecloths, chairs each had a red ribbon tied to them
Invitations	$30	Made on groom's computer
Miscellaneous	$20	Always a good idea to have a little left over for the unexpected expense

Boo! We're Married!

♥

Location: Indoors or outdoors, this will likely be the most memorable Halloween party either you or your guests will ever attend. Find a gathering spot that will suit the size of your party, for instance, someone's home, a barn, a park, really anything that will accommodate the size you need and celebrate the season.

Bride and bridal party: Well, it is a Halloween wedding so the bride wearing black is definitely in the spirit of the theme. A black ball gown is perfect with black eyeliner to match. Long black gloves and a black rose bouquet complete the look. Bridesmaids of course can either wear dresses or costumes.

Groom and groomsmen: The groom would look plenty festive with a tuxedo and cape. For a less expensive option, a black suit and cape would look equally as dashing. Groomsmen can be in similar attire or costumes. For fun, keep vampire teeth handy for some festive photos later.

Ceremony: It isn't just a Halloween party; it's also one of the most important days of your life. Keep the ceremony proper and reception merry. Think about walking down the isle guided by the light of jack-o-lanterns with sound of organ music playing in the background. Once the vows have been exchanged, guests can throw Halloween candy instead of rice and the bride can finally put on the witch hat or cat ears.

Reception: Your centerpieces couldn't be easier, or cheaper. Grab some more jack-o-lanterns and put them on all of the tables which are draped in black tablecloths. More Halloween candy in pumpkin buckets scattered everywhere and guests should be encouraged to come in costume. You can have a costume contest, a haunted house, and serve a standard meal but call it something spooky like Monkey Brains (spaghetti).

Final thoughts: This is celebration where everyone is going to want to bring a camera so make sure you make mention of that in your invitations. This is also a good wedding theme if you know there will be children at the wedding. They should come in a costume and with their pumpkin pails. As the night comes to a close, gather around for some ghost stories and apple cider.

Budget		
The dress	$75	Black evening gown bought on sale, borrowed a wrap from aunt
Groom's attire	$30	Bought black dress shirt, used own tie and suit
Accessories	$10	Borrowed jewelry, bought long black evening gloves

Flowers	$10	Bride walked down the aisle with black roses, groom had rose boutonniere (flowers bought that afternoon)
Pictures	$50	Hired college student, used three friends as well, friend taped wedding
Music	$5	Friend played the organ during ceremony, recorded jazz music played during dinner and reception
Food and drinks	$230	Spaghetti (dinner menu called it "Monkey Brains") salad, and homemade bread were served with red wine, punch, wedding cake, and Halloween candy
Decorations	$35	Jack-o-lanterns on tables, tables had black tablecloths, chairs each had orange ribbon tied to them
Invitations	$30	Made on bride's computer
Miscellaneous	$25	Always a good idea to have a little left over for the unexpected expense

Midday Brunch

♥

Location: A warm spring or summer morning in a park, lakeside property, or church. Guests gather for a morning reception and then meet afterwards for brunch at a friend's house.

Bride and bridal party: A sundress would be perfect for this type of celebration. Something light with a daisy bouquet, simple drop earrings, and soft makeup. The same theme for your bridesmaids, only their dresses should not be white. Instead, have them look for something pastel, like lavender or soft yellow.

Groom and groomsmen: The groom would be just fine in a suit and tie. His groomsmen can wear dress shirts and dress pants with ties, no jackets required. Have them all wear light colored dress shirts and the groom's shirt should be a crisp white. Have the groom borrow some cuff-links from his father or grandfather to add a special touch to his attire.

Ceremony: This is a celebration of your wedding at one of my favorite times of the day. The sun is beautiful and bright, the smell of the outdoors is fresh, everyone will have plenty of energy, and you'll have the entire day to celebrate, instead of just an evening. Try to do whatever you can outdoors. If your ceremony is inside of a church, have the reception outside.

Reception: Not only do I love mornings, but I love morning meals. Your reception food should resemble your favorite breakfast/brunch foods; pastries, orange juice, coffee, fresh fruit, coffee cake, eggs, bacon, bagels, mints, and chocolates. Since it's a special occasion and your reception will likely be mid-morning, almost afternoon, champagne and mimosas are perfectly acceptable. Don't forget the wedding cake! You'll save money on décor too. Flowers are your main expense because they fit the time of year so well. You won't need too many candles or lights. You will need some good music though; something upbeat but not loud.

Final thoughts: One of the wonderful things about this type of wedding theme is the time of day. You'll save money, you'll have the whole day to celebrate, and most importantly- you and your new husband/wife have the chance to get a head start on your honeymoon. Instead of it being ten o'clock at night and you can barely keep your eyes open, you and your partner could be enjoying your first night as a married couple. Wink, wink.

Budget		
The dress	$50	Sundress bought new
Groom's attire	$30	Bought white dress shirt, used own

		tie and suit
Accessories	$20	Borrowed jewelry from mom and sisters, bought new sandals
Flowers	$50	Bride had daisy bouquet, daisies used as décor for reception
Pictures	$50	Hired college student, used three friends as well, aunt taped wedding
Music	$0	Friend played piano during ceremony, recorded music played during reception
Food and drinks	$220	Pastries, eggs, coffee, wedding cake, champagne, and juice were served
Decorations	$30	Daisies everywhere, tables had white tablecloths, chairs each had yellow ribbon tied to them
Invitations	$30	Made on groom's computer
Miscellaneous	$20	Always a good idea to have a little left over for the unexpected expense

Afternoon with the Arts

♥

Location: A theater or art gallery where you can have the ceremony and/or reception. This is perfect for creative couples or for those who crave something original and fun. A venue like this also helps limit your guest list because it's likely that the small theater or gallery will have a strict policy on the number of people it's safe to have in the space at one time.

Bride and bridal party: Anything goes for a dress with this kind of a theme. The bride can make a statement by wearing a bright green dress with gold high heels and red roses. An evening gown or cocktail dress would look great too. Maybe the bridesmaids can wear all black in order to make the brides dress pop even more. Be creative!

Groom and groomsmen: Again, be creative! A place like an art gallery isn't casual but it isn't necessarily super formal. A tuxedo would look fine but so would a nice button down shirt and pants. Maybe a nice shirt, sport coat and fresh denim jeans would be more comfortable. The groomsmen should keep in step with whatever the groom is wearing; if he wears jeans, jeans should be fine for them too.

Ceremony: Chairs lined up to make an aisle with simple flower bouquets and soft music from a music player should suffice. Your ceremony will likely be short but make it meaningful by adding your own vows or reading something special that symbolizes your relationship.

Reception: What is really great about a place like this is the no-cost décor. It's going to be beautiful all by itself and you won't have to do a thing. Spend your money on a nice bouquet of flowers and a few vases for the tables but that's it. Let the venue be the star of your wedding décor. As for music, think of something soft and retro. Ask the venue for use of their speaker system and just remember to bring the music. Food should be appetizers and wine with wedding cake. Appetizers work so that people can feel free to eat and walk around and look at the beautiful art in the gallery.

Final thoughts: The main cost of this wedding is the venue. It may cost a couple of hundred dollars so offset that by using as much as you can of what you already have. Shoes, jewelry, clothes, even flatware and dishes should be borrowed. The theme is "Afternoon with the Arts" but you could do this later at night too and serve just desserts and wine. Either way, this kind of wedding is fun, creative, and definitely unique.

Budget

The dress	$40	Cocktail dress bought on sale
Groom's attire	$0	Wore existing clothes
Accessories	$20	Borrowed jewelry from friends, bought new shoes
Flowers	$40	Bride had small rose bouquet and bought single roses to put in vases on each table
Pictures	$50	Hired college student, friend videotaped wedding
Music	$0	Recorded music played during ceremony and reception
Food and drinks	$200	Appetizers, wine, and wedding cake were served
Decorations	$0	Vases and tablecloths were borrowed for tables
Invitations	$30	Made on groom's computer
Miscellaneous	$100	Payment for use of venue

Meet Me at Midnight

♥

Location: This is one that is ideal for indoors, but it's got to be the right kind of indoors. Consider asking someone for use of their home if it's large enough, rent a room at a bed and breakfast for the weekend (make sure you clear your wedding plan with them first), or use someone's vacation home. Remember, the more intimate the better, the time of your ceremony is unconventional to say the least.

Bride and bridal party: The bride in a beautiful ivory gown with classic jewelry and a full bouquet of something elegant, like roses. A fancy formal gown wouldn't be a wise choice though due to the intimate setting. If possible, have only one bridesmaid. You're going to be in a somewhat small area of space so the more people you have standing next to you, the more it will take away from the personal surroundings.

Groom and groomsmen: The groom could easily get away with a dark suit and an ivory shirt and tie. It would be something formal enough to match his beautiful bride but maintain some comfort. A groomsman could wear the same thing, just with a different color tie. Again, try and have just one groomsman.

Ceremony: Chic piano music is playing in the background as the bride emerges from the top of the stairs or the back of the room. A brief walk down the aisle and the ceremony begins. Lots of flowers and candles with ivory colored ribbons tied to the chairs. The lights should be kept very low and since this is a unique and special midnight ceremony, not a lot of hoopla is necessary. Your guests will never forget this ceremony and will enjoy it all on its own.

Reception: Think of this as a very formal slumber party. After the ceremony, serve champagne and fruit with appetizers for everyone to munch on. Get a pot of coffee going too. Keep some cozy blankets and pillows around and maybe have some romantic movies playing quietly in the background. Think of people finding a comfortable place to sit, with some food and drink in their hands, and enjoying the company around them. At around 3am, the newlyweds can retire to a nearby hotel to begin their honeymoon, and guests are free to leave, socialize, or have an early breakfast at the nearest 24 hour coffee shop.

Final thoughts: If you want to spring for party favors, offer guests travel sized toothbrushes and toothpaste. They'll enjoy the humor of it and likely find it useful at 4am. This is great for a hip younger couple too. If your friends are night owls or you simply just don't want to conform to what everyone else is doing, this could be the perfect wedding theme for you.

Budget

The dress	$90	Ivory evening gown bought new
Groom's attire	$30	Bought ivory dress shirt, used own tie and suit
Accessories	$10	Borrowed jewelry from mom and sisters, used own shoes, bought veil
Flowers	$35	Bride had rose bouquet, red roses used as décor for reception
Pictures	$50	Hired college student, used three friends too, friend taped wedding
Music	$0	Friend played piano during ceremony, recorded music played during reception
Food and drinks	$215	Fresh fruit, desserts, homemade bread, wedding cake, and wine served – coffee too
Decorations	$20	Candles everywhere, tables had dark tablecloths with rose petals scattered on them, silver platters with chocolates were the centerpiece
Invitations	$30	Made on groom's computer
Miscellaneous	$20	Always a good idea to have a little left over for the unexpected expense

Backyard Bash

♥

Location: This is option is perfect for those who crave something informal and also works well if your guest list includes a lot of children. It's simply a large backyard party so think of the friend or family member that has the best set up for this kind of party and ask them if they would allow your wedding and/or reception to be held there.

Bride and bridal party: The bride would likely be most comfortable in something sweet and simple. A sundress or simple gown, probably not floor length. The bride's hair swept into a beautiful braid or bun will be elegant but also practical, especially in warmer weather. Instead of a veil, maybe delicate flowers can be set into the hairdo. The bridesmaids should dress in simple skirts and shirts or similar sundresses.

Groom and groomsmen: The groom and the groomsmen in khakis and white shirts. It might look nice to have the groom where a more formal button down shirt and polo shirts for the groomsmen.

Ceremony: If you can find someone to play the guitar and a soloist, this would be great for your ceremony. Line the impromptu aisle with pots of flowers or ribbons tied to the chairs. Lights of bright colored flowers at the spot where vows will be said and possibly a pergola or gazebo if it can be made affordably or if it already exists.

Reception: Like a backyard barbeque but more special and slightly more formal. Use real plates, glasses, and utensils instead of paper and plastic. Look into the cost of a tent in case of rain and set up small card tables with borrowed table cloths. Ask your friends and family for their card tables and chairs and cover the chairs with inexpensive fabric and ribbons. Each table should have tea lights and small vases with flowers or pots of flowers. Ask some helpful cousins or nieces and nephews to help you serve and clear dishes. Dinner should be grilled chicken or steaks, vegetables, homemade applesauce, and of course, wedding cake. Have pitchers of water and lemonade at the tables or served by your helpers.

Later, set out the cake and some coffee on a buffet table for guests to serve themselves whenever they are ready. Dishes of candy and nuts can also be set out at each table so guests can nibble on something throughout the night.

Final thoughts: This is the kind of party where you may be able to add to the guest list because the expenses will be so little. The outside atmosphere will be perfect for wedding pictures as well. Also, as stated earlier, this might be a good choice if you think there will be lots of children or a group of smaller children (who are notorious for short attention spans and their ability to break expensive things).

Budget

The dress	$50	Casual gown or sundress
Groom's attire	$30	New white dress shirt, used own tie and suit pants
Accessories	$0	Borrowed jewelry from mom and sisters, used own shoes, no veil
Flowers	$45	Bride had daisy bouquet, potted flowers used as décor for reception
Pictures	$50	Hired college student, used three friends too, friend taped wedding
Music	$5	Friend played guitar during ceremony, recorded music played during reception
Food and drinks	$230	Grilled chicken and veggies, baked potatoes, wedding cake, and wine served – coffee too
Decorations	$30	Candles and potted flowers with pictures of the couple were the centerpiece
Invitations	$30	Made on friend of bride's computer
Miscellaneous	$20	Always a good idea to have a little left over for the unexpected expense

Legally Married

♥

Location: The bare bones ceremony at the court house may not sound very romantic but that doesn't mean it can't be. One of my favorite weddings to attend was a friend of mine who got married at the court house with only me and another friend there to witness. After the ceremony, we all drove to a beautiful four star restaurant and had one of the best meals ever. We spent about three hours having dinner and great conversations and afterwards went to see some live music at the bar next door.

Bride and bridal party: The bride wore a beautiful evening dress with her own shoes and jewelry. Her bridesmaid wore her own dress and shoes as well. She carried a small bouquet she had bought that day at a flower shop.

Groom and groomsmen: The groom wore a nice suit and his groomsman wore the same.

Ceremony: The four of us waited for the judge to arrive and the ceremony began with their individual vows and a brief but meaningful statement about marriage and the special day. After, we took some pictures and then made our way to the restaurant for dinner.

Reception: The dinner was fabulous and the restaurant served some of the best food I have ever eaten. It was a French restaurant and therefore the food was served in courses with plenty of time for eating and talking and simply enjoying the special occasion. The restaurant also had a dress code which made the dinner feel formal and really emphasized the fact that this was a special event. Everyone there was dressed up. At the end of the dinner, the waiter brought out a special dessert for the couple and another bottle of wine followed by some coffee. After dinner the bar next door was featuring a great local band and it was a fun way to close out the evening.

Final thoughts: Maybe this seems too low-key for you but if it's your second marriage or you just aren't interested in the typical wedding ceremony or reception, this is a great option. It was truly a special day and will go down as one of the best weddings I've ever attended. It was also one of those weddings that strictly focused on the couple and the start of their marriage. There was very little stress but a lot of celebration. By the way, all of the money saved that evening could go into your honeymoon fund!

Budget		
The dress	$0	Wore her own dress
Groom's attire	$0	Wore his own suit
Accessories	$0	Used own shoes and jewelry

Flowers	$12	Bride had rose bouquet
Pictures	$0	Bride and groom used their own digital camera
Music	$0	No music at ceremony
Food and drinks	$400	Ate at four star French restaurant
Decorations	$0	None
Invitations	$0	None
Miscellaneous	$50	Money for judge

YOUR WEDDING EMERGENCY KIT

For the bride

- o Nail polish and polish remover

- o Tweezers and nail clippers

- o Travel sewing kit

- o Cotton balls and tissue

- o Makeup kit

- o Brush and comb

- o Hairspray and gel

- o Hand lotion

- o Wet wipes and wash cloths

- o Curling iron and hairdryer

- o Bobby pins

- o Toothbrush, toothpaste, and floss

- o Mints and mouthwash

- o Perfume

- o Baby powder

- Deodorant

- Candy

- Extra pantyhose

- Jewelry

- Masking tape

- Travel iron

- Phone numbers for all wedding participants

- Light snack (something that won't stain if you spill it, like fruit snacks or crackers)

- Bottled water

- Tylenol

- Antacid

- Bandages and/or first aid kit

- Feminine hygiene products

For the groom

- Tweezers and nail clippers

- Travel sewing kit

- Cotton balls and tissue

- Toothbrush, toothpaste, and floss

- Mints and mouthwash

- Deodorant

- o   Brush and comb or hair pick

- o   Hairspray and gel

- o   Candy

- o   Hand lotion

- o   Wet wipes and wash cloths

- o   Masking tape

- o   Travel iron or de-wrinkle spray

- o   Phone numbers for all wedding participants

- o   Light snack (something that won't stain if you spill it, like fruit snacks or crackers)

- o   Bottle of water

- o   Tylenol

- o   Antacid

- o   Bandages with a first aid kit

- o   The rings

Other items

_____

_____

_____

_____

_____

_____

_____

LIST OF MUST-HAVE
WEDDING PHOTOGRAPHS

- o Bride and groom (lots of these!)

- o Bride and groom with wedding party

- o Bride and groom with parents

- o Bride and groom with grandparents

- o Bride and her parents

- o Bride and her grandparents

- o Bride and her siblings

- o Bride with her immediate family

- o Bride with her bridesmaids

- o The bride's parents

- o The bride's grandparents

- o The groom's parents

- o The groom's grandparents

- o Bride with the groom and his family

- o Groom with the bride and her family

- Groom and his grandparents

- Groom and his parents

- Groom and his siblings

- Groom with his immediate family

- Groom with his groomsmen

- Bride and groom with flower girl

- Bride walking down the aisle

- Groom waiting at end of aisle

- Bride and groom kissing at ceremony

- Bride and groom walking down aisle after ceremony

- Guests at ceremony

- Guests arriving at ceremony

- Guests at reception

- Picture of bride and groom dancing

- Candid shots of bride and groom getting ready

- Bride looking at herself in the mirror

- Groom pacing before ceremony

- Candid shots of reception

- Shots of speeches made at reception

- Bride and groom cutting the cake

- Picture of the rings

- Picture of the cake

- Picture of the wedding gown hanging on the door

- Picture of the flowers

- Bride and groom leaving the reception

- Picture of the invitation

- Picture of the church

- Picture of the wedding program

- _____

- _____

MY WEDDING BUDGET

Ok, here is where things can get scary but just grab your favorite pencil and go for it. You have to start somewhere right?

ITEM	Estimated Cost	Actual Cost
Dress		
Groom's Attire		
Flowers		
Music		
Pictures		
Cake		
Reception Food		
Reception Site		
Gifts		
Accessories		

Invitations		
Miscellaneous		
	TOTAL →	$

One thing that is not on the budget and depends on where you live is the cost of a license and blood test (if required).

JOBS TO PUT ON
YOUR TO-DO LIST

✓ Find someone to pick up and deliver the flowers

✓ Gather music for reception, borrow CD players

✓ Buy wine and find wine glasses

✓ Make programs for ceremony

✓ Find wedding day jewelry

✓ Get hair and makeup done

✓ Hem wedding dress

✓ Finalize reception menu

✓ Find people to serve drinks and hors d'oeuvres

✓ Make and print invitations

✓ Address and stuff envelopes

✓ Write speech

✓ Borrow silverware and stemware

✓ Find a photographer for the ceremony and party

✓ Find people to help clean up after reception

✓ Buy paper and envelopes for invitations, programs, and dinner menu

✓ Finalize guest list

✓ _____

✓ _____

✓ _____

YOUR GUEST LIST

Write each guest's name, followed by a checkmark in the
appropriate box. For each "NO", move someone up from the
optional list.

NAME	YES	NO

Optional

NAME	YES	NO

Notes

130